Teach on YouTube

How to Start and Grow Education YouTube Channels

Kit Betts-Masters

GorillaPhysics

Teach on YouTube

How to Start and Grow Education YouTube Channels

Subscribe to GorillaPhysics on YouTube.

On my channel I teach GCSE and A Level Physics, but I also talk about education theory and technology.

Visit GorillaPhysics.com and look for the teacher tab!

For Rory and Florence, my little world.

Published by GorillaPhysics in the UK

ISBN-13: 979-8675882182

2020

© Kit Betts-Masters

Contents

I've tried to put everything I know about making videos and making them successful on YouTube in this book. Of course, you may already know some of it! Just like teaching on video, I cannot be sure of the start points of my audience!

Why not have a look over the chapter titles and plot your own way through the book based on what you need most from your own start point.

Otherwise here are some suggested routes through the contents of the book based on some starting points.

From no videos to expert:

1b 1c   2a 2e 2h 2i 2j 2k   3b 3c 3f

Starting with some technical knowledge:

1d 1e   2d 2e 2f 2g 2l 2m   3c 3d 3e 3f

Starting with some knowledge of education online:

1a 1b 1e   2b 2e 2f 2g 2h 2i 2j 2k   3a 3c 3f

Wanting to improve an existing channel:

1d 1e   2b 2d 2f 2g 2m   3a 3b 3c 3d

I really hope that this book will stay with you and will be a useful reference for you as you grow your education YouTube channel.

With this book you can teach anything on YouTube. This book will help you find ways to teach your passion and to share your skills with the world.

Whilst I am a practicing teacher, teaching for specific exams subjects and specifications, this book is for anyone interested in teaching on YouTube. You might be a tutor with skills in any subject! Or just someone who knows a fair amount about a topic that just wants to get started making their own content. In short, this book is for all educators who want to share what they know with the world.

This Book

Goal setting.

Before you start, you should probably know an answer to this question: *What are your reasons for starting a YouTube channel?*

Whatever your answer is, I hope that this book will give you some useful advice to help you on your way.

Don't be shy! It is ok to dream big. There really are normal teachers who have made full time businesses beginning with a YouTube subscriber base that they have grown in their spare time.

Personally I think that any reason to start a YouTube channel is a good one. Here are some which might be at the top of your list:

It's where the students go for explanations.

It's a convenient place to host and share video content.

It's the second most used search engine.

It's a good place to start a business.

You want to be YouTube famous.

Your explanations are better than what exists already.

My own educational channel will be six years old in February 2021. Each February I take stock of the previous year and set myself a new target. At first these targets were based around subscriber numbers. More recently, I've been basing these around the quality and coverage of the content that I am creating. The latter is possibly the more sensible way to set goals for education channels, as students grow up, learners move on. They were never there to consume everything you have to say or every topic you cover in its entirety, in any case.

Probably I started YouTube for all of the reasons above, but foremost in my mind was that it would show me to be the innovative practitioner I wanted to be known as, and that it would help me get jobs later. But the real trigger which made me make those first videos was the students that I left behind in my previous schools, and the statement ringing in my ears; *you can't teach them all, Kit.*

Start now!

Ok, YouTube will probably turn out to be a fad, a generational thing, most social medias do. Likely though it will be the platform that millennials still use when the next generations all get their audio-visual content elsewhere. Teachers making videos and running their own channels will probably not become the norm.

For many young people in 2020 YouTube has become their textbook. It is their first place to answer questions like *how do I…* or to look for explanations for topics that they are studying.

Importantly for you, if you are looking for reasons to start a channel, know that the use of YouTube for education is rising rapidly. Making high-quality audio-visual content no longer takes big budgets and large teams. This decade is a good time to be learning the skills for making videos.

The idea of authorship is changing. Publishing is no longer the reserve of the big publishing houses. We are willing to pay each other for the resources that we create, and students can buy directly from the online teacher themselves. This is all because, like desktop publishing before it, video editing has become something that can be done by the amateur individual, at home, to a high degree of production quality.

Flipped classroom is probably a fad too. Too many people promoted it as a panacea, and too many school leaders denigrate it as leading to disorganised lessons, confused learners and exasperated teachers. (Ironically this is precisely the opposite to what you get when it is done correctly.)

But what *is* here to stay is a new emphasis on student responsibility for their own learning. Students have a vast choice on how to learn a particular topic or skill available. And the idea of delivering foundational, functional content outside of the classroom, in preparation for the lesson, so that more creative things, which deepen thinking, can happen in the classroom, is not a new one.

I write this in 2020 and after the lockdown. It is a time when the number of teacher YouTube channels has grown massively, and when many education brands are recognising the worth of having a YouTube presence to reach their audience.

A change in attitude to videos has come, and it is one which I believe will be permanent. Teachers are more positive about the idea of recording their lessons, we are all more used to appearing on screen and more willing to engage with students out of the classroom. The recent explosion of teacher channels can give a global reach for every education professional who is willing to put themselves out there.

YouTube is where the students feel comfortable watching educational videos. By using YouTube, we are going out and meeting them where they are.

Just like Twitter can give you the scope to network with teachers all around the world, YouTube can give you the scope to teach every young person.

I wrote this book because I want to give you the understanding and the tools to achieve your own goals in starting or growing an education YouTube channel. Whether you are an individual teacher looking to expand your horizons, teach more kids or influence more teachers. Or if you are an education company that wishes to understand YouTube as a marketing tool. I hope you'll find the expertise that you need in this book.

What you should learn from this book.

Many teachers that started making videos during the school closures of 2020 noticed that students didn't always watch the videos they made, or that they started them but didn't stay for very long. I hope in this book to give you some methods by which you can change that.

The goal as a *Teacher-Tuber* is to make engaging content. If your videos are engaging, then people will watch. If your videos are not engaging, then people will pick other videos.

There is no trick to making engaging videos, just as there is no trick to making engaging lessons. They key is to know your audience and to make a relationship with them. This is the same for all social medias. Do that and your channel will grow; you'll reach and audience, influence them and all the opportunities which come from a large social media following will follow.

When I started making videos I thought it would be easy! Then I pressed record, and I got nervous. I imagined myself making the same dry witty jokes as I did at the front of my classroom. I imagined myself having the same easy-going attitude, being the same engaging speaker, on video as I was in front of thirty kids. Ten seconds into my first recording, I knew it wasn't as easy as it looked.

Be glad if you too get the nerves. *Nerves just show you care.* This book will give you practical advice that you can put in place to get over the nerves. It will help you get over the many other stumbling blocks that you will find in your way before you can make that slick looking video that you imagine in your head. Some stumbling blocks are technical, and others are pedagogical, I will tackle both in this book. But believe me; if you are a good teacher in a classroom, you can also be a good teacher on video.

This book will give you advice on how to achieve your goals in making videos. Read, learn and be open. Try the activities they are written to help you put the learning into action. Just like you have to study a video, you should study this book.

What will help you succeed here on YouTube is to get started and take action. Try things out and learn and develop from each step and each misstep. Pull that camera out of your pocket, crack on a massive smile and hit the record button. You're going to love it!

Activity: Spend a bit of time researching your subject or niche on YouTube.

Ask yourself these questions:

What already exists?

What might I do better than what already exists?

What might I do different?

How much time might it take to make a channel like these that exist?

What size of team are working on the channels that you find?

Find channels that you admire and ask yourself if it is possible for you to emulate their successes. Perhaps you cannot do all they appear to be able to do, in which case decide which aspects you can manage.

Make yourself a little mental picture of what your YouTube channel will look like in a year's time.

---

1. Reasons and Goals

1a. My story so far

YouTube is so much fun!

I have published over 600 videos to YouTube, I estimate that I have probably spent around 2000 hours working on this channel. I have spent far more time than that thinking about my channel, learning about making videos and how YouTube works. I am a way off having devoted enough time to it to be world class, but I am on my way. In this book I am giving you my advice from the experience of those hours developing my channel.

Monetarily I have so far gotten little from it. I'm often asked, *why have you not put those hours into tutoring? You'd earn so much more.*

I have two responses to that; *I'm reaching and helping more people through YouTube*, and *I am growing something that I own and that will work for me in the future.*

But really, in honesty, I cannot imagine having done anything else with that time. I cannot imagine not having started a YouTube channel and thinking about how to improve it all the time. I'm a good teacher of Physics, a passable Head of Science, and I enjoy my job, but I love my YouTube channel.

A slow start.

I started making videos because when I moved school in 2015, I felt bad about leaving students that I cared about. School leaders, other teachers, my friends and family said, *you can't teach them all!* But I wanted to!

Other people made success on YouTube look easy and I felt that I could do as good a job or better myself. I thought that it would be easier than it was. I imagined all my old students tuning in and watching, and me still effectively being their teacher! I soon realised that making quality videos was a time-consuming process and I didn't get anywhere near half the course covered.

I thought that it was a good way to present myself as an innovative practitioner to my new school. I wanted to bring new ideas and ambition to a promoted post.

During the Easter holidays before starting my new role I made some simple talk over screen videos:

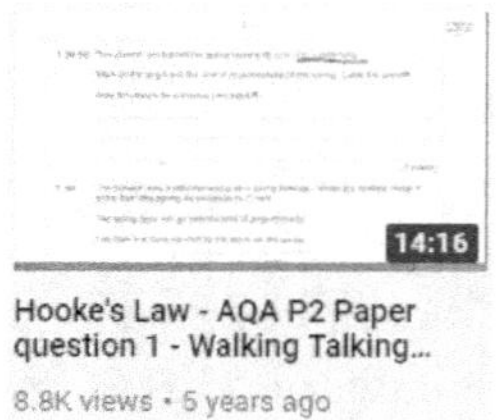

Hooke's Law - AQA P2 Paper question 1 - Walking Talking...

8.8K views • 5 years ago

> *Newton's laws* - had 12 views in its first week.
> *Motors* - had 30 views in its first week.
> *Exam run throughs* - basically none.

This should have been pretty demoralising. I spent hours preparing, filming and editing these videos. What is more, I was pretty sure that the majority of views were my parents, friends and colleagues!

Then this happened…

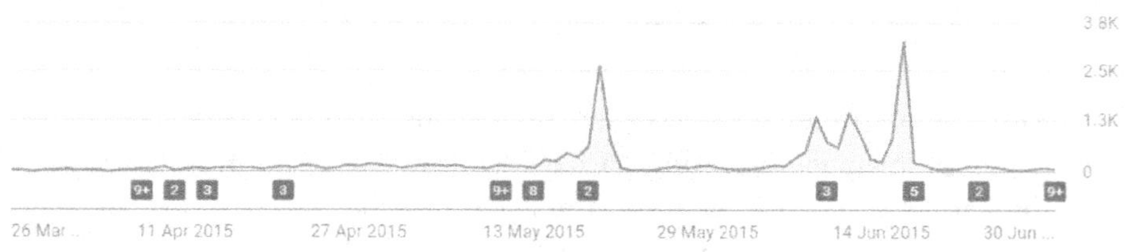

Three thousand views in a day! You see I had hit YouTube gold:

The right video released at the right time.

This is perhaps the most important thing to learn about how to get views to your channel. *Be strategic*; you have to aim for a particular audience who is interested in a particular thing at a particular time.

During the exam period, my hand drawn *life cycle of stars* video got nine thousand views! The excitement was amazing. You see I had hit a niche which was underserved.

There were no good tutorials covering that topic. And so, *my* video on stars for GCSE Physics was the most popular that year.

The very next year views on this video had dried up. There were several videos on that topic… and they were better than mine. The sound on mine was too quiet and I was mumbling! I realised I needed to learn and improve.

At first, don't worry about views, just enjoy learning new skills.

I realised I could achieve my goals, it was possible, I just had to get better at it.

Later than year I met Jen. We were at the same training course at a University and we happened to be on the same table. She looked so familiar! I was trying my best to remember where I had met her before.

Then it hit me, I recognised her from her YouTube channel! *You're the one with the kittens!* I said excitedly.

I had been watching a lot of education YouTube. I was learning about the *Khan Academy*, *Minute Physics*, *Physics Girl* and of course, my two local heroes *Physics Online* and *Primrose Kitten!* Jen said something to me which struck me; *I've got big plans.* At the time she had around three thousand subscribers. I had around a hundred, I think. She was planning to reduce her teaching load to three days a week and use the other two days to grow her YouTube channel.

I remember thinking that it was a very brave decision. Four years later, her business is flourishing, based on her 150 thousand subscribers on YouTube!

Five years later it was me that was recognised at a conference. *You're GorillaPhysics!* They said excitedly and went on to tell me how much they and their students appreciated the videos. I cannot tell you what that moment meant to me. I certainly felt justified that I hadn't gone for the tutoring option!

Trial and error.

I tried loads of different things over the next few years. Vlogging was a bit of a dead end, (everyone wanted to be a vlogger in 2016.) Although *a day in the life of a teacher*, sounds good and it got a few clicks, to be honest, it's not something my audience was interested in.

Early on I tried to learn the technical aspects of making videos. I tried everything, I consumed videos on how to make YouTube videos, from script writing to techniques like green-screen and special effects.

The YouTube *Creator Academy* lessons are good. So too are YouTube tips and strategy channels like *Think Media TV,* with Sean Cannell, and *Video Creators,* with Tim Schmoyer. You can look far and wide for advice on how to make YouTube videos and how to get them in front of your audience. There is loads of advice on how to grow channels for all the popular niches on YouTube. If you want to make entertainment, lifestyle vlogs, make-up tutorials, or a gaming channel for example I feel that you are really well served with advice on how to do that and do it well. There isn't much out there specifically for education channels though, and that's why I wrote this book.

"Good enough" production value.

I realised that there were many things that I was doing that I didn't need to do. There were many tips which are important to travel vlog channels or comedy channels, but not so much in the education niche. For example; I now understand that click bait titles are less important for education channels than titles optimised for search. And I now understand that a two-camera set up with professional quality cameras are more important for corporate videos, and one camera with good enough editing is fine for an education channel.

I learned that there is a production value which is "good enough" for education channels. It's worth discussing what I mean by that as I will talk about it quite a lot in this book.

"Good enough" production values simply refers to a video which is of a high enough technical quality to not have that be the reason for the viewer abandoning it. "Good enough" usually comes down to three things:

- *The camera isn't too shaky or rapidly moving.*
- *The person or scene is well enough lit so as to be visible.*
- *The sound quality is clear and loud enough to not cause any strain or annoyance.*

Many education videos, which would otherwise have been useful teaching materials, are ruined by not having one of these things right.

I learned that you should be trying to make the best videos that you can, but you shouldn't let overreaching for high production values stop you from making clear, concise and accurate explanations which meet the needs of a group of students.

Reaching more people.

The next exam season I discovered the benefit of using live streams. In fact, to give your channel exposure and increase the watch time on it, there is very little better that you can do than a well-timed, high-quality live stream. You see YouTube will promote a live stream more than a recorded video during the time which it is live and shortly after. It will, for a day or so, be much nearer the top of any search which it appears.

I ran a series of live streams in the run up to the 2018 exams. Demand for exam specific videos was very high during this time. These videos were usually an hour or so long, and although they took a long time to plan, they took zero time to edit. They aren't perfect, they aren't always slick, but they sound good and they contain very useful details. They have become some of the most popular videos on my channel they perform well partly because of the excellent start they got, being popular when they were streamed. We call this type of video "evergreen" because it stays relevant and gets views year after year.

Every Core Practical in A Level Physics (Edexcel) - GorillaPhysics - Level Physics Revision Live

GorillaPhysics - Grade 9 and A* Physics · 17K views · 2 years ago

Also, if you like GorillaPhysics and want to help me shape and expand my channel and resources, why not join my Patreon community and become part of Gary's squad:

For most of them I had no more than 30 people watching live. But the positive thing for the longevity of these videos is that most of them stuck around for most of the video. This is one of the key signals to YouTube that this is a video worth promoting.

A pre-recorded video could take weeks to accrue 30 hours of watch-time, but these had got it as they were being filmed! I learned that total watch-time is one of the most important metrics for YouTube growth.

On top of this, I was engaging with a core group of students during the exam period and linking to and recommending lots of my other videos, in this way I was sending people directly to *my* videos, which is another great signal to YouTube that this is a channel worth promoting.

This is a strategy that I will be using year in year out during the exam periods, it's hard work but it's so rewarding. In the 2019 exam series, twenty thousand

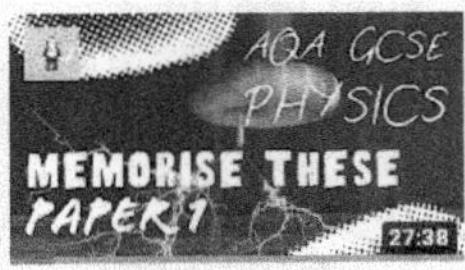

AQA GCSE Physics - Paper 1 - memorise these - the night before the exam

GorillaPhysics - Grade 9 and A* Physics · 30K views · 1 year ago

Here's a summary all the bits you need to have ready to go for AQA GCSE Physics Paper 1 on Wednesday. Here are some useful playlists that might help as well. Energy:

students tuned into my live stream *the night before paper 1* and this half hour of teaching online has become one of my most popular videos.

Be consistent.

One thing I have never quite got right on my channel, which I am looking to put right this year, is covering the specification in a consistent high-quality style. I've probably covered everything somewhere in my 600 videos, but all my videos are different, because I like to try new things and learn new skills.

My advice to anyone starting an education channel would be to, decide early on a production method which is manageable in terms of time, but high enough quality that you will still be pleased with them in the years to come. As quickly as possible make a "good enough" video covering every part of the specification(s) you teach.

This way as your channel grows, and you make the extension, or exam skills, or study technique videos, you can be confident that students discovering your channel know that you have something quality covering everything that they need to know for their exams.

My channel now.

Where I am with YouTube and *GorillaPhysics* now is that I feel that I have the knowledge to make my channel a big success, but I struggle to find the time! This is frustrating and I'm very aware that I need to make YouTube a manageable part of my life. Balancing my full-time job, my family and making videos could easily lead to burn-out.

Burn-out is a major issue for YouTubers as, for many, their channel is a passion which sits alongside other full-time work. This means that thousands of YouTube channels are started every day, but many are left, unloved with only a few videos, with very few views to show for them.

Very enthusiastic starts are made every day, but the reality of YouTube is that getting to milestones like a hundred, a thousand, ten thousand subscribers is hard work. It takes consistent grind, attention to quality and careful reflection on what you produce and how it is going to help you reach your goals.

I have to keep everything in perspective. Everything needs to be the right size in my life. I need to focus on all my professional and personal commitments in my life and not be consumed by making content for YouTube.

I've loved the journey so far. And I'm probably at the end of the beginning of that journey. I tell you all this because I want you to be realistic in your own expectations of what it will take to reach your aims. I want you neither to get consumed by running your channel, or to give up on it!

I look to the massive success stories, to keep me focussed on what is possible with education on YouTube. I look to the constant positive feedback that I get from the young people who watch my channel. And I enjoy the way my videos look and sound. These things keep me going and keep me passionate to grow my education YouTube channel for years to come.

1b. Why you should try it

Build a community around your purpose.

Before you start YouTube, have an answer to these questions:

Who is your audience?

What is your purpose?

What do you hope to achieve?

The answers to these questions will help you keep perspective as you work on your YouTube channel. If your audience grows less rapidly than you thought it might, you can check back with your expectations. If your videos start to take off and you feel like your life has been taken over, you can give yourself a reality check!

The first two questions are about who your videos are for, and why they should care! If you cannot answer these then your channel will fail.

In each of your videos you need to explain to someone watching that they have found the right place. That person is likely to be sitting privately, studying. You don't necessarily need to say it in many words, but your content should convey a feeling. They need to feel that; *this content is made for me.*

If you convey to that one person that this is the right channel for them, they will consume every video that you have to offer. However, if they feel that your content doesn't meet their needs, the next time they are shown your video, they will choose one of the others that are shown alongside it.

When you explain your purpose to your audience you begin to build the most powerful thing for YouTube growth: a community around your channel.

Where audience and purpose meet is where you should build your community.

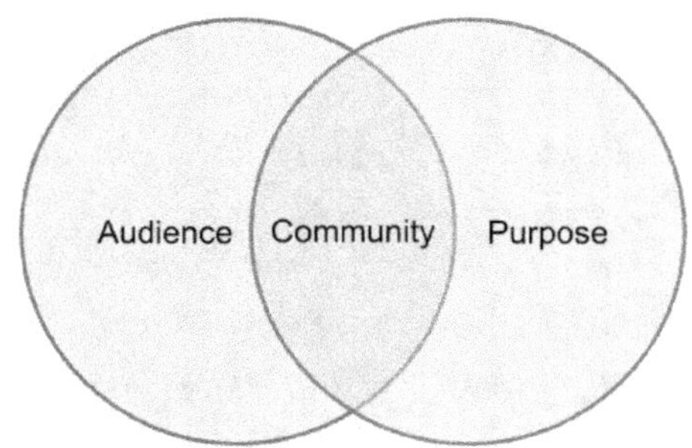

Get your targets.

The third question is about setting goals. Dream big but be realistic.

I reset my goals every February, simply because this is the month I began YouTube. Usefully it's also the month where things start to pick up towards exam season. I have not met my goals every time. But each year, my goal is what makes me put in the hours in front of the video editor, and keep thinking of new ideas, and keep analysing the successes and failures I've had so far.

Remember that you are unlikely to get your targets overnight. Education videos rarely go viral! (Especially those specifically for a specific exam course.) In the chapter "YouTube Strategy" I will go into how you can write a content strategy to ensure that your videos are discovered and promoted by YouTube. I will also give you a way that, should you be aiming for millions of views and subscribers, you can try and make viral content.

With consistent uploading, over several years, you could reasonably expect to earn a meaningful supplement your income. On top of this you will find your videos such a useful resource for your own classes. And I am sure you will get the reward of strangers who will take the time to thank you for all your efforts.

Enjoy the anonymity and monetise when you are ready.

The nice thing about not having many views at first… is that no one really notices your mistakes! Being relatively anonymous, you can enjoy learning the skills whilst no one is really watching! 😊 😃 🙈

It will probably take a long time to become monetised. The current threshold for joining the YouTube Partner Program and being eligible for advertising revenue is 1000 subscribers and 4000 hours within the last year. You also need to have a good standing without any copyright or community guideline strikes.

You may see advertisement next to your channel and in front of your videos from day one, however. As this is because YouTube has the rights to display advertisement on any part of their website.

If you have aspirations to earn money directly from YouTube advertising then you'll need to be working towards this goal from the start and make sure that you have intellectual rights over your content and that you are making content suitable to be advertised next to!

When you pass the threshold to become monetised you will not suddenly have a life changing income. Education channels are unlikely to be the most lucrative of channels for advertisement income. This is because educational videos are generally aimed at a demographic which don't tend to have a large disposable income! If sole concern is to make money, consider a channel niche aiming at the lucrative 25-35 age range.

As such, even though most of my videos are monetised, only around 20 percent of my playbacks have ads shown next to them!

Early in the development of your channel focus on learning your craft, and think about revenue later when you have a channel size which can command views. At this point if you wish to you can plan to make content with a commercial focus. For example, my highest earning video is one in which I explain how a heat powered stove fan works. Although this video is meant for an audience of young people learning physics, it gets a lot of views from people interested in buying one of these! Because this video happens to have an audience of potential buyers, advertisers are interested in placing their ads next to it.

Strategize from the beginning.

If your goal is to make a massive income and completely change your lifestyle, *this is possible*. But it will take two things; a consistent strategy which you execute with perseverance, and a channel identity and value proposition which will appeal to a larger audience than just your subject and the qualifications that you teach.

Channels which make the mega bucks will usually be those that offer entertainment value above educational value. If you want to achieve a huge subscribership, and a million views on every video you put out, you need to have mass appeal. By creating a channel which teaches young people specific content, for specific public examinations you are limiting your mass appeal.

There is a bit of a paradox here, because it is easier to get a YouTube channel started if you have a narrow niche. But the narrower your niche the lower your chances of becoming very popular. There are fewer videos made for very specific topics, so there's less competition. There are fewer potential viewers so there are fewer opportunities to be discovered. Every video you publish to YouTube walks this line between *volume* of potential viewers and *competition* for those views.

My advice if you want to go big would be to start with a narrow niche and widen your appeal once you have a channel with some weight of subscribership behind it.

Find reward in the people behind the numbers.

If your aims are more humble though, you should know that there is real joy in providing value to students beyond your classroom and your school.

Remember to think about the individuals who are taking the time to watch your content. If your video only ever gets thirty views, that's another class you've helped. If you video gets ten comments, that's ten people who have appreciated what you've done enough to write you a message of support. If you reach one hundred subscribers, that is one hundred actual humans who have thought *I like this person and want to hear more of what they have to say.*

Do that and you have the opportunity to build a platform for yourself to have a larger influence than you would by simply teaching your classes. There is the opportunity to be noticed, and perhaps have the edge over another applicant for the next job you want. There is the opportunity to build some skills which will become more and more useful as education embraces video. There is the opportunity to be at the forefront of the changing ways that video can be used to communicate and educate.

With skills in video you can use video beyond how it is being used today.

You can, as I have, build an income which contributes to your salary, just as much as a head of subject role might. Or you can, as others have, build a business which your YouTube influence allows you to promote directly to students, families and schools.

You can be glad that you are helping people who are looking for the best outcomes in examinations.

---

*Activity: Why are **you** going to start a channel?*

Be honest with yourself, if your goal is to make this your sole income then it's going to take hard work and a determination to match your ambition. If you're just in it to help out a few people and use your resources in your teaching, then you don't need to beat yourself up about the statistics in your journey.

Set yourself some long and medium-term goals to revisit as your journey progresses.

1c. Making your first video

Let's get started!

To get started making educational videos we're going to follow a simple recipe. Feel free to embellish as you gain confidence with the medium! Follow the sections in this chapter and in a couple of hours you will have a good YouTube video which *will* get views on your channel!

I suggest that you use your phone for the whole production, as this activity is really about finding your own voice on video and learning the process. There is more about gear, shooting and editing in later chapters which of course you are welcome to read first. But if this is your very first video, keep it low jeopardy, follow through the process so that you learn the workflow of making a video.

You should end up with a short video which is "good enough" in no more than a couple of hours. Once completed upload it and share it, there are details about how to do that in the technical bits sections.

Above all, crack a big smile! Making videos is fun and the more you can relax and be yourself on camera the better the outcome will be.

Pre-production.

Write a very short script entitled either *how to get an A* in A Level (your subject name)* or *how to get a grade 9 in GCSE (your subject name)*. Think of the type of advice that you usually give to your class, something specific to your subject but which underpins success in you subject's exams.

If you don't have a subject specific channel, then perhaps change the title to something along the lines of *how to study effectively*.

Aim for no longer than 3 minutes, so like half a page of A4 10pt text. It's worth scripting exactly what you are going to say when you are a beginner, but later you can get away with just outlining what you are going to say.

Download a video editing app to your phone. I use *adobe premiere rush* and *kinemaster*, and I have used *powerdirector*. *iMovie* on the *iPhone* is also good. Check it loads ok, and ideally have a little play with some of the features. Many apps like this have a short tutorial taking you through the basic features. The free versions are absolutely fine for now.

Think if there are any useful props, particular diagrams, photos or images that will help you illustrate your point, bring them to the production session!

Filming.

When shooting your video there are three important things to get right; *lights, camera, audio.* You don't need any extra gear here; we're going to cheat on all three and just use our phones!

Don't worry if it takes more than one take to get it right. If you mix up your words just, pause, and carry on from the start of that sentence, you can edit out the gaff later.

- **Lights**: You need to make sure plenty of light falls on your face when you talk to camera. We're going to use natural light instead of studio lights, find a window and face it. Ensure the camera is between you and the window and lots of diffuse light is falling on your face. If possible, turn off the lights in the room behind you so that you are nicely separated from your background.
- **Camera**: It's important that the camera is steady, so don't film handheld if you can avoid it. If you have a little phone stand, or selfie stick maybe use that, or just prop up your phone with some books! Spend a little bit of time framing yourself so that your face is nice and large in the screen, maybe a medium shot, from the navel up. Film the video in landscape format rather than portrait, at this is normal on YouTube. Try to have the camera at eye level, so that you avoid showing more nostrils than eyes! Make yourself comfortable, sitting or standing. Briefly consider what is in the background, preferably not a messy pile of papers or unmarked mock exams, I use a gorilla! If possible, use the main camera on your phone, rather than the selfie camera, it tends to be a better quality. And this will also mean that you look into the lens rather than at yourself in the screen!
- **Audio**: Sound quality will put viewers off more than video quality so ensure that you can be heard easily. Do this by making sure that there is as little as possible background noise and by standing as close as possible to the camera. For example, don't film at school during lesson change over; turn fans off, turn the projector off, shut the classroom door, or the windows. Use your normal classroom voice, not a shouting voice, but not a chat with a friend voice either. Present to the camera like you are talking to one person who is listening attentively, but be loud, clear and animated.

Editing.

The guiding principles for editing educational videos are; make it snappy, make it visually appealing, and make sense.

Use the snipping tools to trim off any fat, any long pauses, any sighs, or any long *sooooo…* sounds you make!

Use titles to add key text, or emphasis to important points. This is where all your awesome PowerPoint skills come in, just think; *what information do they need to see?*

Add images, pictures, even overlay video if you can shoot some cut-scenes which make sense. Consider adding a background music track; but keep it quiet enough so that you can still be clearly heard. Avoid drums or lyrics in any background music, and don't bother if you think it is too distracting.

Later in this book there is a more detailed explanation of the editing process, as well as some advanced editing techniques. no need to skip forward now unless you were finding the simple editing wasn't achieving what you wanted it to.

Export, share and evaluate.

Watch it, ask yourself if there is anything quick you could do to improve it, a little extra clip, a photo example of what you mean, or anything to add a little bit of fun. Then export it, probably go for a 1080p setting which is normal HD tv resolution, but 720p is also fine, (higher if you have a wiz phone and want to show off!)

Plug your phone into your computer and save the file, or upload straight to YouTube from your phone. Then evaluate and enjoy thinking of the next idea!

If you are looking for inspiration you could find my video *3 Easy Ways to Start Making Educational Videos.* I talk through how to make videos using tablets, PowerPoint or by using talking head videos. You could also skip ahead to the "Types of Video" and "Categories of Video" chapters in this book for more advice.

3 Easy Ways to Start Making Educational Videos
GorillaPhysics - Grade 9 and A* Physics • 393 views • 3 months ago

These are the easiest ways to make an educational video. I have three ideas in this video to get you started teaching on videos in a matter of minutes! I know you are going to like the third! I...

Activity: Get started by making your first video using nothing but your phone following the recipe in this chapter. Once You've done this either evaluate it by watching it back and thinking what you're going to do next time, show it to a friend go to your class and ask them to honestly answer these questions:

1. was everything you said clear on first watch?

2. was the pace of your speaking voice too slow or too fast?

3. was anything in the video distracting or made it difficult to follow the explanation?

4. did you feel confident the speaker was an expert about what they were talking about?

If you like what you've made, then skip forward to the "technical stuff (YouTube)" section and get your first video public.

1d. What is YouTube?

It's like videos that anyone can make and share isn't it?!

YouTube is a place where anyone can make videos and share them immediately on the internet. But what YouTube is now in the 20s is very different from what it was, and what it is trying to become. Knowing these things will help you to find your place on YouTube and to change with it in the future.

YouTube is also a search engine. It is the second most searched search engine in the world… behind Google. And remember YouTube is owned and managed by Google.

YouTube is also a social media, a traditional media, and a prime platform for advertisement, product placement and influencer marketing. It is a place where gamers stream content, educators educate, but it's also a place where misinformation is shared, where grooming for terrorism takes place….

But YouTube is also one of the most rapidly growing platforms for educational content. It has a very young audience and is for many the first place they look for advice, instruction and education.

YouTube is changing. It is no longer a repository for amateur phone videos of funny pets or silly dances. Those videos have found other places online, (think *vine* then *tik-tok*!)

Traditional media outlets are recognising the reach of YouTube and are ploughing big budgets into creating content just for the platform. Big businesses recognise the influence that YouTube channels can have over people, (but they are struggling to understand and exploit it!)

Despite this there is still room for the little independent video creator to make a popular channel with millions of views. This is because YouTube doesn't mind how much was spent on the video, or if one person wants to watch it or one million people want to watch it. Both videos have a place on YouTube.

YouTube is also an AI algorithm which is constantly seeking to link viewers with video content that they want to consume. This AI is learning all the time and getting better and better at linking video to viewer.

Typical YouTube videos.

As you embark on your YouTube journey understand that there is a certain type of video that viewers expect on YouTube. This is different to what they expect on *snapchat*, or *tik-tok*, and different from what they expect from *Netflix* or *Sky*.

YouTube viewing is somewhere between casual consumption, flicking through a news feed on a small screen in vertical orientation, and the settled home cinema session sitting down for hours in front of a large TV screen.

Videos on YouTube are typically between 5 and 15 minutes long, and they have a "good enough" production value. They are usually consumed on a smartphone, tablet or laptop, in horizontal orientation, in small snippets of leisure time.

People do in fact have long attention spans and will binge watch content if it provides value. But they will make up their minds quickly whether they have found a video which offers them what they were expecting, and they will leave.

YouTube videos are all about making an interpersonal connection between the creator and the viewer and delivering as much valuable information in as short and easily digestible package as possible.

The YouTube algorithm follows human behaviour.

YouTube is a machine geared to keep people watching, and if you can learn to make videos that people will *click on* and then *watch through*, no matter what your budget is, YouTube *will* promote you.

Sure, Will Smith can walk on and have a million subscribers within the week, but little old you can also get there, it will just probably take you a little longer.

Above the machine-like algorithm, that pumps out videos to a highly engaged audience, using their patterns of what they search for, what they watch and how long they watch it for, there are real human connections at the heart of the platform. Think about the individual person that is watching your video and try to make sure that *you* are engaging *them*.

YouTube is upfront about how their algorithm works and why some videos get suggested and get more views than others. But the advice is always that the machine tries to learn what the humans want, and what their behaviour indicates they are most likely to enjoy. For that reason, don't try and learn tricks, or make videos that you feel the machine will promote. Instead make content for the humans and let the machine learning follow their behaviour.

Activity: Create a channel name.

Your channel name is easy to change later so don't feel precious about it. Take your time over it and don't settle for your first idea. Spend a day thinking up short snappy names as you go about your business. Say them out loud. Try them out on a friend or partner. Have a laugh about possible names with some of your students, anything to try out lots of ideas before settling on the one that best fits your channel.

A common YouTube teacher channel name is your surname followed by your subject so for a long while I was MrBettsPhysics. And if you really have no better ideas I would suggest you start with that!

But try and pick something that's going to be descriptive, potentially searchable and have some indication of the character of your channel.

I picked my channel name because it was something different to what was already out there. It's the very antithesis to the corporate type of channel which I'd never be able to create on my own. With hindsight I wish I'd settled upon a channel name which had some indication of my unique selling point which is for students aiming for the highest grades in GCSE and A level physics.

I didn't get my name right at first and I often revisit the naming and branding of my channel as my time on YouTube continues.

1e. Is it click bait?

The importance of titles and thumbnails.

Whether you like it or not getting your videos watched on the internet today is about competing for a click.

You need to see the two most important things to do this as being your title and your thumbnail.

Your title is what will make the video appear in a student or teacher's search for a topic. The thumbnail is what will give them the confidence to click on your video above another.

Put together, the title and the thumbnail of the video are the two cues that the *person* who is going to watch *your* video has to make that decision. Get it wrong and they will watch a different video.

Write for people not the algorithm.

It's really tempting to blame the algorithm for your videos not being shown to people. It's really tempting to feel that the channels with the established audiences, or the budgets to allow them to advertise, are always going to appear higher in search or to be suggested more often than your video. But this is simply not true.

The algorithm will promote videos which get *clicked* and then get *watched*. For this reason, every decision you make around your channel you should be aiming to compel that *person* in your audience to act.

Write titles, descriptions and tags to convince the humans in your target audience of the quality of the content of your video. Design thumbnails to get the attention of those human beings that you are looking to reach.

If you aim to please the robot which makes the decision to present the video to that human, you will end up making no sense to the person who decides to watch the video. They will not click and so the robot will not promote you.

The algorithm is always geared to follow the behavior of the human consumers of the content. Therefore, a video that is clicked on more often and watched for longer is much more likely to be presented to a user in search or in their suggested videos.

Perfect titles and thumbnails.

So how *should* they look? What *should* they say?

There are no hard and fast rules, but my advice would be to experiment early on and then try and build a consistent style based on what you find works.

Ideally thumbnails will be all of these things; *eye-catching, descriptive, professional consistent, brightly coloured, trustworthy, approachable*.... But they can't possibly be all of these things. The best advice then is just to make them fit with your channel.

The most common advice for thumbnails is to feature a close up of a smiling human face, and to tease something of the content of the video. If you have text you need to use just one or two important words and make sure they are legible even if the thumbnail is shown very small.

I've found that what works best for me is bright colours, very limited text and some background image representative of the content of the video. For example, for a video with a calculation about the speed of a train I might have *calculating speed* in red over a still frame from the video of the calculation.

For a small education channel; a title which is very close to a phrase that someone might type into a search engine is generally more likely to get your video in front of the right people. But that might not be the best way to convince someone to choose that video. Adding an enticing "click-bait" element to the title might encourage them to pick that video over another offering the same content.

Many channels see their titles as having two halves, one optimised for search, one to entice the viewer to click. This is a good way to go, and you'll see this quite a lot on my channel. Importantly make sure your titles are accurate descriptions of the content, and that they fit with the message of your channel.

Activity: Do a search for some keywords in your subject, for example ... ask yourself which video you would pick.

What is it about their title and thumbnail that makes you want to watch it? What can you learn from their titles and thumbnails that fit with the purpose and audience of your channel?

Go back and change the titles and thumbnails of a few of your least well performing (but not totally dead) videos.

The deeper meaning of your channel.

One favourite channel of mine is *Story Greenlight*, where Jeff Bartsch, who has been an editor on massive budget films and TV shows, discusses the importance of storytelling in keeping people glued to your content.

He talks about the Hollywood vehicle for keeping viewers engaged in films and says that this is a powerful vehicle for creators at all levels. They call it *the thing under the thing.* If you think about any movie that you love, and think about why you love it, I'll bet it's because of some deeper meaning you get from it.

The thing under the thing refers to the deeper meaning in your content. The subtext which pervades all of your videos. *The thing under the thing* is often unsaid but which is known to viewer and creator alike.

For my channel it's about helping motivated young people through the minefield which is secondary education in the UK, to help them get the top grades.

If you want a reason, if you want a goal, then my advice is to try and find your *thing under the thing* as early as possible. And try and weave this thread throughout all of your content!

I'd definitely recommend finding *Story Greenlight* as soon as possible and to find your own *thing under the thing* as soon as possible.

Deeper meaning is precisely the opposite of clickbait. Clickbait implies a style of title which is intriguing and appeals to our *need to know* facet of our brains, but then a video which has none of the content promised. Searching for that subtext which will engage your audience achieves the same thing; i.e. the click; but rewards the viewer with the deeper meaning. This will mean they seek out your content time and time again.

Activity: Go to an education channel that you admire.

What does their channel look like? What do their thumbnails look like?

What is their "thing under the thing" and how do they ensure that it pervades all their content?

Make a few design decisions and try to use them consistently for your channel art, your thumbnails and in the content of your next ten uploads. Revisit this later and ask yourself if you are conveying the message that you set out to convey.

---

2. Technical bits

2a. Technical stuff (YouTube)

Setting up your channel.

Sign in to YouTube. You can use an existing google account or make a new one, but I'd recommend using your own email address rather than a school or other work account. This will be the email address which is used for future verification or password resets. You can choose "for myself", or "to manage my business". You are now logged into YouTube as a user, but you do not have a channel yet.

Make a new channel by clicking either the option "create a channel" or "add or manage channel" from the dropdown menu from the circular icon in the top right of the browser window.

I recommend not using the default "personal" channel that YouTube automatically creates for you as it might be difficult to collaborate with others later on in your channel development. Also, it will be a channel which has your name as the channel name, and might not want that!

Give your channel a name. There's no need to be precious as you can change it later. I strongly recommend something that is likely to be individual, but which also represents the *purpose* and *deeper meaning* of your channel.

The next step is to upload a profile picture and describe your channel. This profile picture is your logo and is displayed prominently next to everything that you do on YouTube. Again, you can change it later, or just upload a quick selfie. Write a short and simple description including key terms that you expect your prospective to audience search for. Include your *value proposition* and why people should subscribe.

If you intend on making a particular type of educational content, or content for particular exams, describe that here.

Add your social media links; for example, your *Facebook*, *Twitter* and *Instagram* profile links. Think carefully about these if you only use these platforms for personal use. There is no need to link an *Instagram* account if it has no relationship to the educational content that you make on YouTube!

If you have a website for your brand add it here as the first link.

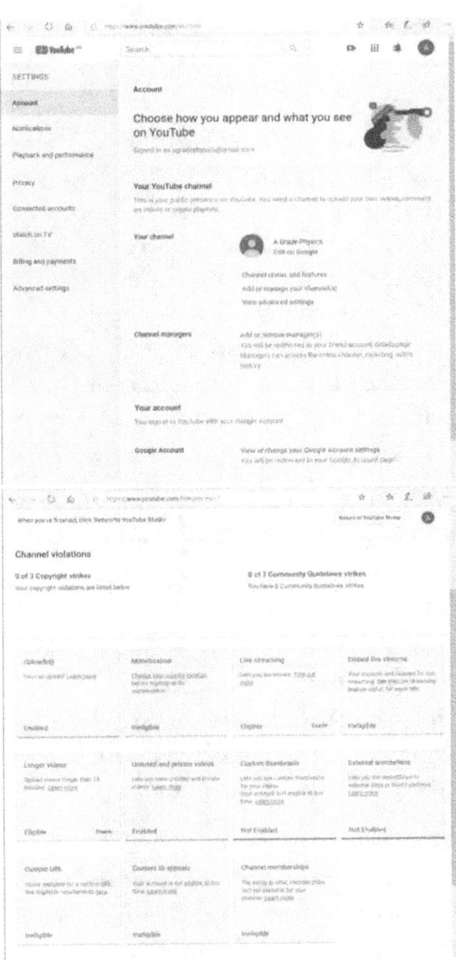

Next you need to go to "settings" then "channel status and features". During the life of your channel you can unlock all of these, but you'll not be able to do some of them at first.

First step is to verify your channel by entering your phone number and receiving a verification code. All this means is that YouTube knows that they actually have a human who made this channel and so they will not get jammed by robots uploading hours and hours of footage! This unlocks custom thumbnails, videos longer than 15 minutes and livestreams. You'll want to be doing all of these. Other features such as monetisation will not be available until you reach certain milestones on your YouTube journey.

This is a pretty important page to know about as it is where you'll see notifications of any copyright or community guideline strikes, which can affect the features that are available to you, including stopping you publishing videos altogether!

Next you need to customise your channel. Go to the YouTube studio, which you can find by clicking on your profile pick. Notice you are now in a different part of YouTube; at "studio.youtube.com".

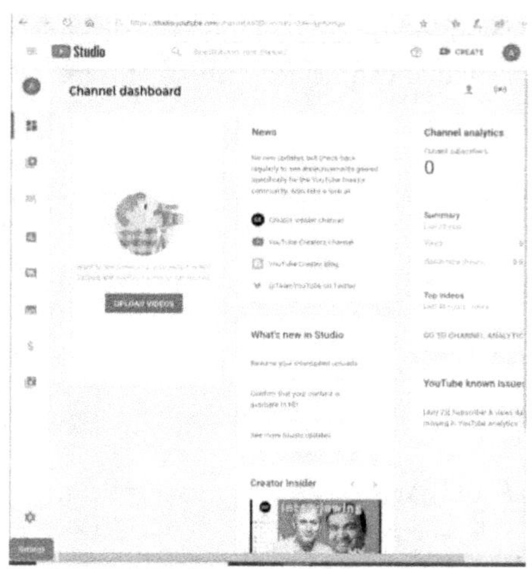

This is where you manage your channel, rather than the website you go to to watch videos!

The cog at the bottom right is "settings", go there and then to "channel" then "customise channel".

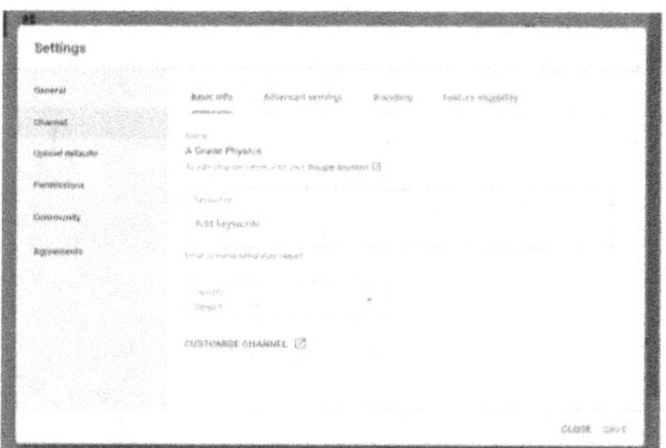

The first creative job is to make your own channel art. The channel art is simply a photo which gets cropped to different dimensions depending on the device that the person is viewing on. It's worth taking a few moments to make sure that the channel art conveys a sense of the *value proposition* of your channel.

Search for YouTube channel art templates and you will find blank files with the right size frames for you to add some text and images. There are even websites that will automatically generate you a set of channel art files that you can upload to your channel for free. You can do this step later if you wish, in which case choose one of the sample photos and move on!

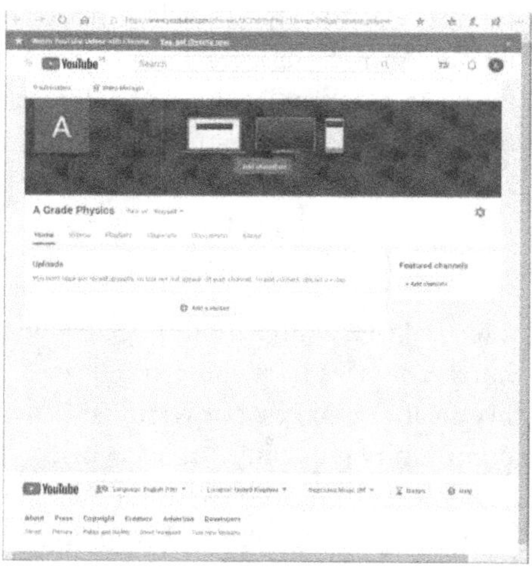

This "customise your channel" page is also where you pick what videos and playlists are shown on your channel homepage. This is important for education YouTube channels as you want to organise your content so that it can be navigated through in a logical manner.

You can choose to display playlists, important videos, even a channel trailer which automatically plays when someone visits your channel for the first time. You will see that links are displayed over your channel art and other channels that you subscribe to are shown down the right-hand side. In your tabs initially you will not have tabs like "community" or "shop", as these are features which can be enabled later as you pass certain milestones in YouTube growth.

You can also add details and links in your "about" section. You can add a business email address, just know that this email address is visible to everyone. So it can be found by bots! I have my kit@gorillaphysics.com email address up. (Feel free to reach out by the way.) And I am not inundated with spam, so you need not panic. Just maybe don't use your personal or school email here. You can add a location here as well.

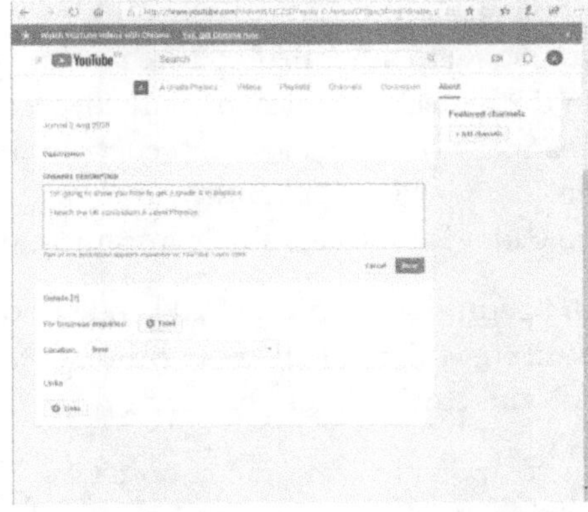

Next let's explore the YouTube studio. And go to "settings/channel" again. In "basic info" you can add channel tags. Go for around five to ten here, that are common for all of your videos.

Then go to "branding". You want to add a water mark which sits at the bottom of all your videos. You can use your profile pic, or some prompt to subscribe. Normal practice is to have it starting at five seconds in.

Then go to "advanced settings". You need to specify whether your channel is made for kids. Remember for YouTube purposes "kids" means under 13. So, if you are aiming at exam age students, click "not made for kids".

"Upload defaults" is a very powerful SEO tool. You can set the default visibility of your videos to "private" or "unlisted" so that you can preview and optimise each video before you publish it for everyone to see. You can add quite a lot of detail here of things like links to your social medias, general search phrases, and later links to popular videos and playlists of yours. Remember that you are writing

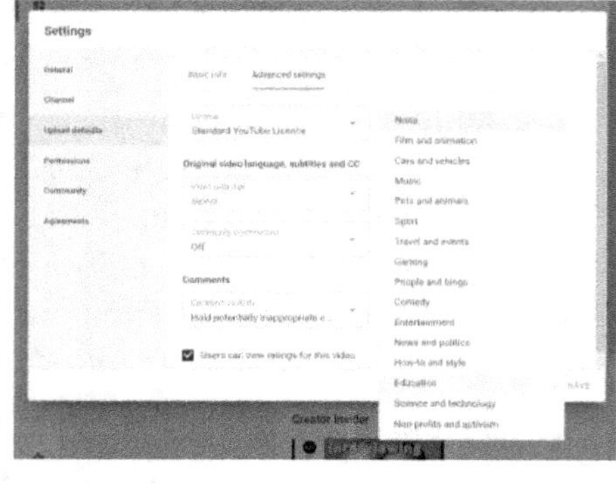

to the humans that watch your videos, not some robot which will scan your channel. You can add your general channel tags here. Add anything in your upload defaults that you would want to be in the metadata of every video you upload. (Metadata is all the information that accompanies the video.)

In "permissions" you can add and remove managers and moderators if you want to work with other people on the channel. All you need are their Google account email addresses.

In "community" you can choose how YouTube moderates the comments section. I strongly suggest that you allow comments and ratings as they are good indicators of quality to YouTube. You should encourage participation and engagement from your audience! But here you can have the option to block certain words, or comments that include links. I have had very few incidences of abuse in my time on YouTube, and rarely has it been persistent. If there is someone you wish to just hide the comments of you can just type their account name into the "hidden users" box and no one will see their comments on your videos. YouTube also has the same report abuse features that you'd expect to see in any online chat space. It's very easy to mute, hide or block people.

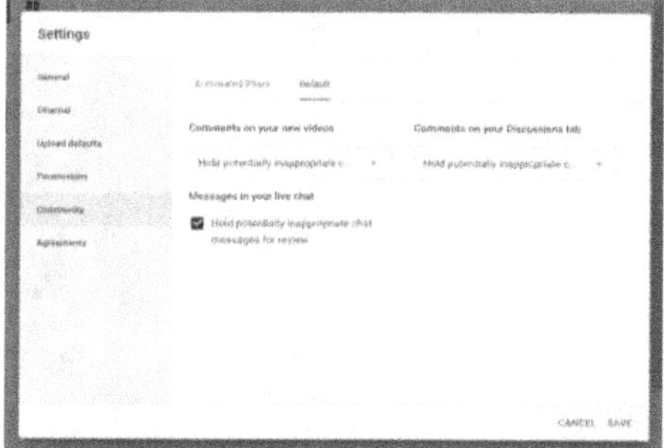

I also have "hold potentially inappropriate comments and messages for review" on for all sections, as this just means that YouTube will filter out any swear words or spam before it gets shown on the video comments section. Generally I like things to be open on the internet, but as your audience may be young people it's better to know that there aren't going to be offensive words used directly under your content.

You can also see your channel ID and make yourself a custom URL should you need them later in your YouTube journey. I recommend that you wait before you do this anyway as you cannot change the URL once you have made it if you decided to change your channel name.

When you are ready, you'll find the little plus video "create" symbol in the top right of your channel homepage or YouTube studio. You can go ahead and upload your first video or just be brave and go live!

If you haven't made your first video, then go ahead and do it by following the recipe which I have written in the chapter "making your first video!"

A typical upload.

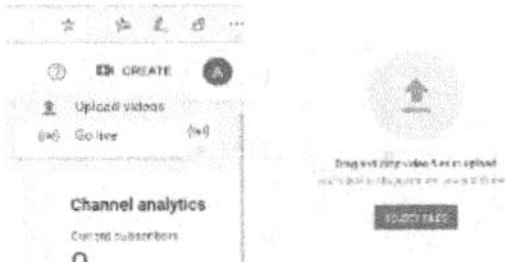

You'll find the upload video button at the top right of your YouTube browser page. You can drag and drop your video(s) into the panel here or select them from your folders on your computer.

Once you have started the upload, you'll see this screen, which you can work through inputting the metadata for the video. YouTube will continue uploading and then processing your video.

You can change the title and write a description here. Remember that you are writing to encourage humans to want to watch the video, but you are also trying to optimise them for search. You do this by including key terms and phrases that you think people are likely to use in search. There's much more about this in the previous chapter "Is it clickbait?"

The title and first few lines of description are the most important things to get right for both appearing in search and to entice a human to actually decide to watch your video.

"Upload defaults" are a good way to include any key terms or information about your channel that you want to be displayed in the metadata of each and every one of your videos. As a minimum include your channel value statement, and any other social media links that you wish to be associated with your YouTube channel. If you have a website, this should be linked in every video description.

It is very important to use custom thumbnails. YouTube will select a few thumbnails from your video, these will typically be a still from the video where either there is a person smiling or there is a large title on the screen. These might be ok, but YouTube will be less likely to promote a video without a custom thumbnail as it indicates that it is content being made without care and professionalism!

On your thumbnail include around three bold words and any images which give an accurate clue as to what is in the video. Use a human face where appropriate. Use bold but consistent colours.

Add the video to a playlist. Playlists are a great way to organise your content on your channel homepage.

You must specify if the video is made for kids. (It isn't unless it is aimed at under thirteens.)

You should also add tags that are consistent with the content of the video and the search terms that you are targeting with your title and description. These are not as valuable for search and discovery as the title and thumbnails are so don't spend ages over it!

Set the "video type" to Education. In "upload defaults" you can also pre-select like not made for kids, and education video.

You should leave comments on in my opinion. YouTube's filters do a pretty good job of holding rude comments and spam for review and you can view these and block the very few abusive people you will come across in your time on YouTube.

When your channel is monetised, you will see the monetisation options. I'd suggest that the ads options are all ok except I find the overlay ads really distracting and convey the wrong vibe for an education video. People who watch YouTube are used to having "skippable" and "non-skippable" ads, before after and during videos, so I think that those are fine. In my experience the majority of ad revenue comes from "skippable" ads, so definitely leave them on. You can choose to have "mid-roll" ads on videos over 8 minutes, and ads at the end. YouTube will try to place them at natural breaks in your video or you can manually place them.

The monetisation audit is where you state whether your video contains things that advertisers would not be keen to be associated with. I'd be surprised if there was anything like that in an education video! YouTube will also automatically scan your video for anything that it expects is not suitable for adverts. You can appeal for it to be reviewed by a human if, for example, something of legitimate educational worth, maybe a nude painting, or a dubious line in a poem causes a demonetisation flag against your video.

Once your video is uploaded and public you can start the conversation with a pinned comment. Something like *watch this next to understand more* or *ask if you have any more questions you would like answered on this topic.* Even just *let me know if you found that video useful* is a really useful way to encourage other people to comment!

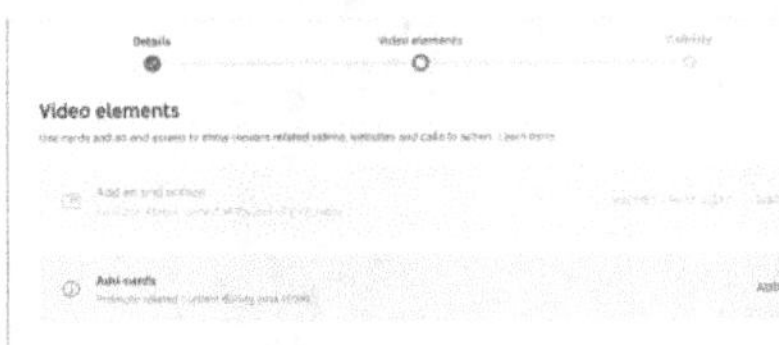

In the video elements section, you can add cards and end screens. The end screen is where you provide a link to a video or playlist that you think the viewer should watch next and a button with your channel logo to encourage them to subscribe to your channel. Cards can be placed to appear in you video and can promote a variety of things, usually videos and playlists. I'd add all five of these that you can, but be aware that they are taking people away from your video before it is completed. This can impact your watch time and so the likelihood of YouTube recommending your video! Try and put cards towards the end of the video and at natural points where you recommend other videos for the viewers to watch.

Visibility is where you chose who can see your video. I would suggest always making your video "unlisted" at first. This means you can see the video if you have a link and you can schedule it to become public at a later date and time. As you learn about your audience, you'll learn which are good times to publish for your channel. In my experience students tend to search for educational videos on

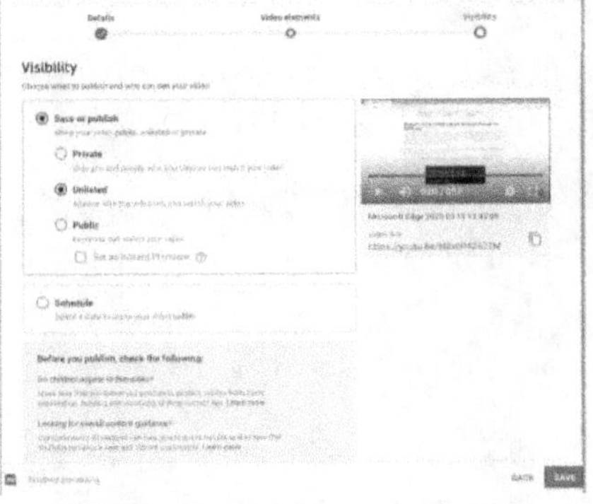

weekday evenings. YouTube studio now has a feature in which you can see when your viewers are most active. You want your videos to get as much watch-time in the first day as possible, as the algorithm bases a lot of decisions about your content on the initial viewing figures and audience retention.

At any point in the upload process you can save your upload as a draft. So, don't worry about getting it right first time, and take the time to reflect on and re-draft the most important parts of the metadata; the title, the thumbnail and the description.

Activity: Follow this checklist for your next upload.

1. Write a descriptive but enticing title, including any keywords that you think someone would search to find this video.

2. Write a description which also includes the keyword phrases that you wish your video to appear in searches of. Also elaborate on the content that the viewer should expect to find.

3. Design and add a custom thumbnail to your video.

4. Add your video to a relevant playlist.

5. Schedule a time for release when you think that the video will have the most chance of being viewed. I usually go for weekday evenings during school term times.

6. Share the video on all of your social medias.

7. Add an end screen with your subscribe icon and one or two relevant videos from your channel.

8. Add cards towards the end of your video, using custom teaser text if the titles of the videos aren't likely to get the click.

9. Complete the monetisation audit if your channel is in the YouTube partner programme. Do not click made for kids unless your video is aimed at under 13s. Remember that this is primarily to avoid channels trying to market inappropriate products to young people which is probably not what you are doing!

10. Enable comments and write a pinned comment, which either encourages others to comment, or provides a link to whatever the call to action was in the video.

Live feeds.

Live streams are the easy way to the top of search. During the time which it is *live,* YouTube promotes a live feed above many other videos for related search terms. Because of this they are definitely something that you should consider when building your channel from scratch. YouTube does not want your live feed to have no viewers so you can count on the algorithm to try its best to connect you with an audience! Live streams then sit on YouTube just as a normal upload would and will continue to get views.

My suggestion to you would be to do live streams after you have made, and are happy with, a few normal uploaded videos. There are two reasons for this. One is that you'll feel more confident on camera and the second is that when people who discover you live visit your channel to decide whether to subscribe, they will see a working channel with videos that should interest them.

Think carefully about when you live stream. If you are targeting teenagers then a live stream on a Sunday morning in the summer holidays will have no one watching. Whereas a live stream the night before a public exam will have hundreds of students dropping in.

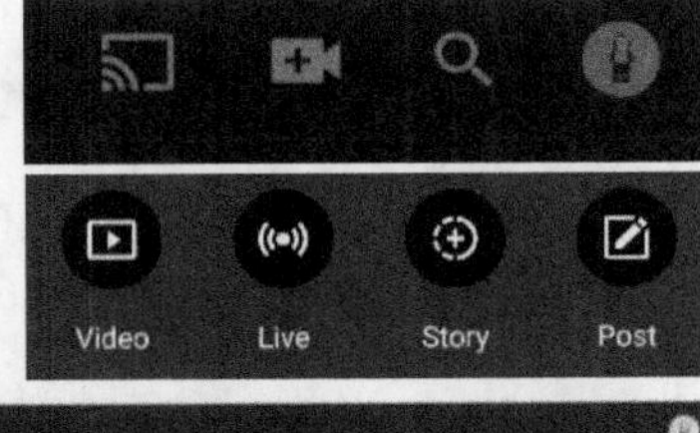

There are basically three ways to go live; on your phone through the YouTube app, in the browser through a webcam, and lastly through a broadcast programme.

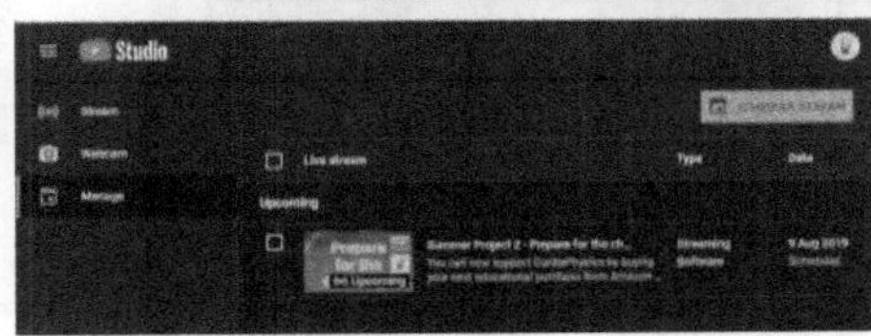

The first two options will be no challenge for you to set up. The quality will be like a video call or an online meeting. The chat covers part of the screen and you can interact with it on the phone in real time, muting people or responding to live questions.

There's nothing wrong with using these easy methods to stream live content, just be aware to schedule the stream and set it up with titles, thumbnails and descriptions just as you would any other upload.

But be aware of their limitations. You should use this if you just want to pop up for a casual chat. You can choose between different webcams that you may have connected, or which microphone to use for best quality. So, you could, for example stream from a visualiser and a USB microphone should you wish.

Using a broadcast app like *Open Broadcast Studio (OBS),* (which we all use because it's free and does everything), gives you far more control over what your stream looks like. It takes a little bit of learning but it's a very capable programme.

OBS communicates to your channel by entering the stream key and stream URL in this "stream" section of the live stream tab in YouTube studio.

I'll talk about exactly how to do this in the chapter "Technical Stuff (gear)" chapter where I discuss various software.

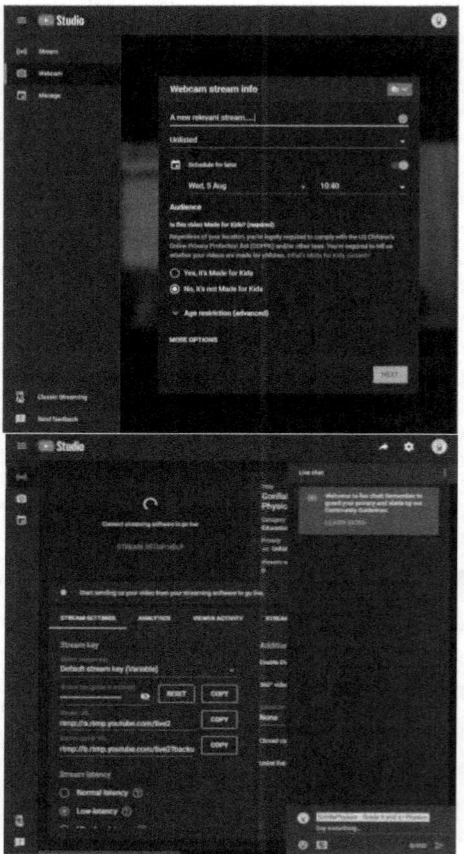

Tube Buddy.

Tube Buddy is the browser extension that I would recommend everyone gets, even if you are only going to use the free version. I'll tell you about some more useful browser extensions and websites in the chapter "understanding search and discovery online."

There are many useful things that it adds to the YouTube website and studio. For example, it will suggest tags and keywords as you type then. It will allow you to make changes to the metadata of many videos at once so and it will let you name custom thumbnails quickly in the browser.

Usefully *Tube Buddy* points out best practices on YouTube in the right place and time so you can put them into action.

There's loads that it can so for you so install it and read about it to find out!

Copyright.

I chose to use "Man on the Moon" as a song over the credits for an early YouTube video I made. After a few weeks the video was taken down and I received an email about copyright from YouTube. It told me who the claimant was, *Sony Music* I believe, and that I had the opportunity to contact them and ask their permission. I did and they responded, but they retained the rights to advertise next to my video.

This process is automated now, and if you use music, images or footage that you don't own you are more likely to get a notification that you cannot monetise the video, and that someone else may get revenue from the video. It now gives you the option to cut out the section with the copyright material right in the YouTube studio! Leaving the copyright material essentially means that you do not have all the rights to your own video. I would recommend that you avoid this as far as you can.

You may be used to indiscriminately taking images from Google image search for your *PowerPoint* presentations in school. Largely this is not a violation of anyone's copyright, as long as you aren't selling that resource or claiming that it is all your own work. However, you need to be a little more aware of copyright on YouTube. Anyone could see your work and make a legitimate, (or perhaps even malicious,) copyright claim.

Google image search has a very useful tool which lets you filter for copyright information. Bear in mind though that Google listing the image as "labelled for use with modification" is no guarantee that

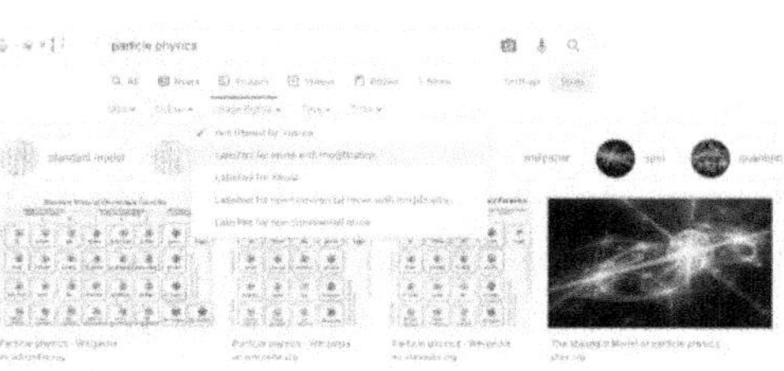

it is copyright free. It is best to always check the source of the image and read the details of the image licence. Even if they are in the creative commons, the images may require attribution within the video itself or in the description. Whilst this is easy to do, if you use many you may find it becomes a bit of a pain to remember to link to the source page for every image that you use.

Use the YouTube music library, you'll find it in the sidebar of YouTube studio. It's a very large database of simple music which you can use with no worries about ever having copyright strikes or monetisation claims against your video. The music there isn't going to win awards, but you'll find a jingle, or backing music or sound effect that you like in there that you can use with no worries.

For images and stock video try using free stock sites like *pexels* and *pixabay*, you can find quality still photos and short video clips there which are free to use and royalty free with no attribution required. Or try looking for free stock footage at places like the *Internet Web Archive*.

I would strongly suggest that you use your own diagrams and images. Making these will mean that you build up a bank of images and other resources that you can keep using as your channel develops.

Sometimes you can find images which are listed as public domain, or creative commons in the *Wikimedia Commons Library*. But always read the licence, some images require you to give credit to

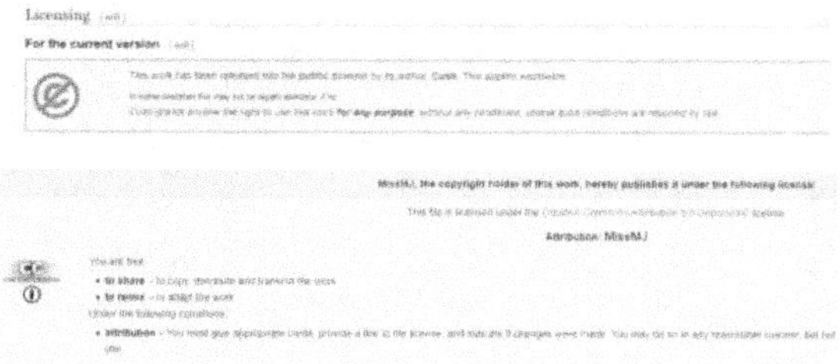

the copyright owner, or that the work you make including it also has to be shared under creative commons. The majority of images that I use are created by myself, but where I wish to use something that exists already it's usually from *Wikimedia* or a free stock site.

Poor standing in copyright strikes will also mean that you are unable to monetise your content. This may not be important to you now but it's a skill that is worth learning early. Good practice around copyright is a habit that it's best to get into whilst you develop your channel. It may not be that you wish to monetise your videos now, but you may wish to monetise them later.

Take pride in what you create and take the time over it to make it all your own work. Make it a habit to use your phone to take photos or videos of work that you do in your classroom. Collect diagrams or notes that you make on your board in your classroom, or images of models you have made in school. Use these images to illustrate your videos rather than relying on Google search to be your first port of call for any images you need.

Monetisation.

Nope, sorry, YouTube is not going to drive a van full of money up to your door after the first few uploads!

To monetise your videos, you need to enrol in the YouTube partner program. This will take time as you need over 1000 subscribers and over 4000 hours of watch time in the preceding year. To get to those milestones will take not only time, but competently applying the skills that I've introduced in this book. Focus on getting those bits right before you worry about making money from adverts.

In any case, a channel just barely qualifying for the partner program is not likely to earn large enough amounts from advertising to make a significant impact on your life. For this reason, don't prioritise monetisation early on when you are starting your YouTube channel, rather prioritise developing the skills and understanding of the way that YouTube works. Prioritise learning the skills for making compelling videos so that you are ready to take advantage of monetisation when you eventually reach a size large enough to benefit from it. Look upon monetisation even when you do pass that threshold as a small reward for your hard work getting there.

There are other ways to monetise though. Many youtubers sell merchandise, that's just things like baseball caps or hoodies with your logo or slogan on. I'm not sure that really fits well with the teacher YouTube channel but perhaps posters, pens and notebooks are something that you could make and sell. Currently there are many models of making products which do not require you to make or keep an inventory. These channels are called *print on demand* or *drop shipping* providers. Essentially you design, they manufacture and distribute in exchange for a large share of the profits.

To make any large amount of money by selling merchandise you are going to need a much bigger following than you're likely to make early on in your YouTube teacher journey. However, if you did want to give it a go then there are several options, for example *Teespring* is a very popular one, as is *Amazon merch*.

There are also several ways that you can promote items to your audience and earn money when they buy using affiliate marketing. The most common affiliate marking is the *Amazon Associates Programme*. This is a good option because of the vast and varied nature of what they sell. But you could approach other companies which fit into the educational niche and value proposition of your channel.

With affiliate marketing essentially you earn a small percentage of the sale when a buyer is referred to a website via your affiliate link. This costs the customer nothing extra and you don't need to handle any goods or shipping. Just be careful to recommend products that actually make sense to your audience and try to promote them in a natural way where they actually make sense in your content otherwise you will lose the trust of your audience.

The most successful way that I've monetised my YouTube channel is through writing educational materials. I sell educational books using the *Amazon Kindle Direct Publishing* print on demand platform. My books are available as a *Kindle* book and as paperbacks. They are specifically targeted to areas of physics that I didn't think were well served by textbooks and revision guides that are published by traditional publishing houses. These sell quite well, and I have more books in the pipeline

If you choose to monetise your channel in this way, just be aware that it can be fatiguing for viewers to feel like they're constantly being sold things. Initially you should focus on building an audience that trusts you and trusts your advice about your subject. Then bring in a higher value option that they can choose to pay for to get more value than your videos offer for free.

Remember why your audience have come to your channel, and make sure that your monetised offering fits with their expectations. In short, your ways of making money should be the same value proposition as your channel, just more valuable! Keep your audience in mind first and foremost and think about ways to turn your channel into a business later.

That being said, if you have the time, selling a few hats and t-shirts with your logo on is perfectly fine as a bit of fun!

There are ways to charge for your videos. YouTube has a membership option, which viewers can decide to become a member rather than simply a subscriber. This is only available to channels that have greater than 100,000 subscribers. You can give certain perks or videos that only your members can see. It costs the viewer £4.99 each month. I would suggest that this is a monetisation option for channels with large followings which are aimed at an adult audience with a disposable income.

You could also set up a pay wall website, where you can list your videos within areas of the website that only viewers who have paid to have a login to watch them. This again will work best if you have a large following. To make a success of this you need to be sure that both your free material on YouTube and the material that they are paying for is of the highest quality.

I would suggest, for most, a business model where your videos are free but that you advertise some premium feature which offers the same value proposition, just more valuable. In this way you get the benefit of YouTube promoting your videos to everyone it thinks will watch them, and you can be advertising and linking to your educational products. Perhaps your paid login website uses the free videos but has self-marking entry and exit quizzes for each one. Or perhaps there are downloadable worksheets to go with each video, or a way to track their progress through the courses that you teach.

Patreon is a way you can create a membership like experience for people wishing to back your education channel, as is *bymeacoffee.com*. On these sites you are essentially asking for donations to your channel. Patrons can donate via one off payments, or choose to subscribe to a regular payment, perhaps in exchange for some backstage access, or other perks that you can offer.

Monetised channels can also earn money through "superchats", these are messages in the chat of a live stream which are paid for by the user. They are instantly promoted to the top of the chat and highlighted. Students sometimes use these to ensure that their question in a Q&A session gets answered. Again, I would suggest that these are revenue streams worth exploring, but that you need large numbers of viewers with disposable income to watch your streams live.

2b. Accuracy matters

Making too many mistakes will cost you.

Educational channels need to be a credible, trustworthy source of information. Students are not going to trust a teacher who makes errors regularly.

You need to establish be a trusting relationship with your audience. Everyone makes mistakes, but if you appear to have knowledge than the people you are trying to teach, then your videos will not be chosen by people when they appear in search. Your videos' *click through rate* (CTR) will be low and YouTube will not continue to promote your videos.

Correct errors you make using editing. If you got something wrong, accept that it is something that you are going to need to film again. A quick voice over, or an asterisk with a note on screen, can sometimes cover cracks

For this reason, you need to ensure that you thoroughly research your topics, that you are up to date with the latest assessment information, and that the information you provide matches the level of the qualifications you are teaching. Be strict in yourself and take the time to get things right. Do this and students will trust your channel to tell them what they need to know and be more likely to select the video on any given topic from your channel rather than the competition.

If you have an error pointed out to you, there are lots of ways to deal with it, the only way *not to* deal with it is to ignore, or even hide the comment. Respond to the person and agree with them if they are right, challenge them and explain if they are wrong.

For major mistakes take down the video and re-record it. For small errors like slips of the tongue, or perhaps you say one thing but the text on the screen says something correct then you can probably get away with leaving it. You could use a card which pops up at that point in the video though, or you can use the YouTube editor to snip out the section with the error, (providing the video makes sense without it.)

At the very least, pin a comment to acknowledge the mistake. That way when the viewer looks down in the comments to point out your error, (usually in a kind public service kind of way rather than a gloating *you flipping idiot* kind of way,) they will see that you've already been made aware and have addressed the error.

Who is watching?

My last point about accuracy, is not about making mistakes. But is about accurately knowing where the students are up to. There has been a great deal of work recently gone into the sequencing of our curriculum. You can have no way of knowing what students do and don't know when they meet your video. But you *can* address this by calling forward or calling back to what is coming next, or what they should know before they watch this particular video.

Just try not to presume what your viewers already know. Try to avoid phrases like; *you'll have been taught this, you'll have seen this demo* or *your teacher will have told you*. Try to eliminate the words that convey that you think they already should know what you are teaching. *Obviously!* This can be very disconcerting for the students who have searched for this video because it wasn't *obvious* to them!

One common reason that students search for videos on educational topics on YouTube is that they didn't get a satisfactory explanation of something from their teacher, tutor or lecturer. Or at least this was their perception of the explanation. They need to feel that *your* explanations are better than what they have had so far on the topic of the video. For this reason, plan and sculpt succinct, accurate and well sequenced explanations rather than just hitting record and waffling on as you make notes on screen. For these students, if you are not more competent than their teacher, they probably won't be back for more. If you are a confident accurate explainer, then they will recommend you to their friends and your channel will grow organically.

You can become their trusted teacher. Teach with a consistent and engaging style and make your explanations accessible and accurate and they will come back to you for the next explainer video that they need.

Derek Muller from the channel *Veritasium* discusses how videos can lead to misunderstandings. His PhD thesis which you can find easily by search, (it is called *Designing Effective Multimedia for Physics Education*,) goes into much more detail on the style of video that he has popularized. Look at his channel and you will see that the videos begin with a commonly held misconception.

Essentially, he has found that where videos just taught a concept, explaining it from start to finish, students retained misconceptions that they had before they watched the video. Whereas where a video started with a misconception and then challenged why it was wrong, students more effectively retained the correct conception when quizzed after the video.

2c. Types of video

Deliver valuable content in a "good enough" production value.

The most important thing to get right on YouTube is to create content with value. If your video doesn't provide value to an audience, it will fail. Keep this foremost in your mind as you create your content.

It matters less what form the content takes than whether your audience gets value from it. You will be a success on YouTube if you create something that engages people to watch, and they will do so if they feel that they are getting the value you promised in your titles and thumbnails.

You will fail if your content does not provide some form of value to an audience. No good idea, high production value, or fancy edits will paste over the cracks of content which has not been made with the interests of the audience at heart.

I'm going to talk about the three main "types" of video here. By "types" I mean the video format and the production technique. It is important to remember though, that the content is king. I'll go on to talk about the content of educational videos on YouTube in the next chapter "categories of video".

There are lots of "types" of video; livestreams, studio sets, vlogs, comedy skits, songs, talking head, chalk board, multiple camera or interview style, to name a few. You can also have fun with "green screen" effects, making conversations with yourself or other fun video effects; there are any number of creative ways that you can make videos. You'll find more on these more creative ideas in the chapter "Advanced Video Editing Techniques".

In this chapter I'm just going to stick with three "types" of video, which are likely to be the core production method for most education YouTube channels. You'll find here a simple list of what you might need to achieve each type of video and what a cost might be for "good enough" production value. You'll find much more explanation of gear, what it is used for and what it costs in the chapter "Technical Stuff (Gear)".

I'm going to presume that you already have some type of computer or tablet which you can use, so have not accounted for that in the cost.

Type of Video	Talking Head	
What you need	Your Phone or any digital camera made in the last decade! (Look for minimum full HD). A tripod! (preferable) an external Mic of some kind, (lavalier or shotgun.) Lighting solution (video lights, or big window!)	
Cost for "Good Enough"	£100 ish (You can go mad here though.)	

This is the most common type of video on YouTube. And for good reason, it is a classic production style which leads to an engaging viewer experience when done well. It can also be made for relatively low budgets and can be made in a time efficient way when you get used to the workflow. My pro-tip here is to plan lots of videos and batch record them, then batch edit them later.

For education channels this is a great way to deliver study tips or general wordy information. You can overlay words or key points, maybe cut to key diagrams or short video demonstrations, but this can lead to a lengthier production process.

Remember to talk directly into the lens and not to be tempted to look at the image of yourself on the screen as you talk. You need to have lots of light falling on your subject and a good microphone as close as possible to your mouth.

It takes a bit of time to relax on camera and be yourself, but you can do it!

Type of Video	Voice Over Presentation or Screen Recording	
What you need	*Open Broadcast Studio (OBS)* or … Record Slides in *PowerPoints* or … Record Using *Zoom/MSTeams/Google Classroom* or … Screen Recorder on any PC, Mac, *Android* or *iOS* tablet (A USB mic will give you better quality than the on-board computer mic.)	
Cost for "Good Enough"	£0 providing you already have a PC or tablet.	

This form of video for beginners is the easiest way to get satisfactory results. For example *Microsoft PowerPoint* has a built-in video creation tool which many teachers will feel really at home using.

This is the best way to deliver lots of information in a short space of time, and once you get good at it you can create videos of this type very quickly.

There are loads of great apps on iPads or other tablets that let you record the screen as you make notes with a stylus or flick through a presentation. For me the best way to make this type of video is through OBS, which I talk about at length in the chapter "Technical Stuff (Gear)".

Many people struggle to keep a flow of speaking at the same time as capturing the screen or making annotations. My pro-tip here is to consider recording your voice over separately from your slides, making annotations or capturing your screen.

Types of Video	Voice over Hand Drawn	
What you need	Visualiser (or other solution to get a top-down visualiser shot.) (Preferable) OBS software to capture visualiser and webcam simultaneously. (Preferable) USB Mic (although some visualiser or phone mics are very good.)	
Cost for "Good Enough"	£200 ish (Or you can use your phone with a top down mount and either screen mirroring or recording video in the phone.)	

For me the greatest value of a visualiser is using the same materials and equipment that the students are using to model what they are going to have to do in your subject in exactly the same way as they will do the task.

You show how to correctly use equipment like calculators or geometry equipment, or even just demonstrate the way they should set their work out on the page in their books. This is especially valuable when it comes to modelling how to solve the problems posed by exam questions. It is effectively like you are showing them the same view that they have of their desk in front of them!

Done well this "type" of video is powerful and engaging. My pro-tip here is to either use editing, or to prepare the resources in advance, so that viewers do not have to spend ages watching you write when you aren't saying anything.

This "type" is a good one to try because it is a very natural way to present, especially given how familiar most educators are with a pen and paper! You can use software to capture your webcam and visualiser simultaneously.

"Types" of videos in action.

I suggest that you learn each of the three types of video and get good enough at making them, because they each lend themselves to videos with different purposes.

My educational content comprises broadly of three video formats:

- *I use voice over presentation, or screen recording, for tutorials.* I teach a specific topic within the specifications that I offer, sometimes over a *PowerPoint*, a visualiser, or with in class demos of the Physics that I am discussing.
- *I use a visualiser for exam technique videos.* These videos will usually be centred around an exam question or set of exam questions. I am trying to demonstrate how to solve the problems posed by the question and the content teaching is incidental rather than focussed. I exemplify what's in the mark scheme and I point out common errors.
- *Study skills or revision tips are usually talking head videos.* I add occasional text on screen to emphasise points and to grab and hold attention.

I also sometimes make "specials". These are often videos which satisfy my own interests rather than the interests of my audience. I am not precious about them and I am not disappointed if they are not popular. But they are important because they are meaningful to me. These are usually where I try out and learn more creative video production techniques. You can find out more ideas on interesting and creative video styles in the chapter "Advanced video skills and techniques".

Listen to what your audience like and react to the trends on your channel. If you do some talking head videos to try it out and you find that they are way more popular than your voice over videos then make more in that style. If you find that when you try and use presentations you get requests to actually see you working through the questions, give it a go!

As your channel develops you will find that your audience ends up being quite like-minded to you! This is the self-selecting nature of YouTube audiences. They engage with the personality in front of the camera. You may find that one video is unexpectedly popular, and this may open up follow-up videos which may give exposure to your channel to a much wider audience.

Activity: Make a simple 3-5 minute explainer video using this simple recipe.

Set aside a three hour block of time where you can work without interruption. Try and stick to the timings given and complete the video in no more than three hours.

Decide before you start what which of the three types of video production from this chapter you are going to use. Decide which microphone and camera or computer/tablet for screen capture you will use. Decide which editing software you will use and what computer or tablet you will use to edit your video. You don't want to be using your time figuring out technical details during the three hours for this task.

***30 minutes.** Do your research. Look at your favourite textbooks, watch any videos that already exist on your topic. Answer these questions in your research: What prior knowledge do viewers need to access this explanation? How is the topic normally explained? Are there any key diagrams or analogies which are always used? What is the key fact that you need to hammer home in your explanation?*

***10 minutes.** Outline your video. Think carefully about the sequence of your explanation. Make sure that you are not trying to cover too much in one video. Try and cover one thing in as short a time as is possible whilst being sufficiently detailed so as to be accurate.*

***20 minutes.** Write a script using voice recognition on MS Word or Google Docs. (If you don't have this available, just ensure that you write in the way that you would normally speak). Begin by telling them what they should know by the end of the video. Include an indication of what they should already know before they start. Include a repetition of the key point at the end. Read it back, cut out any unnecessary chat. Ask yourself if it will sound natural read aloud.*

30 minutes. *Record your voice over. Do this into the best quality microphone that you have. Have the mic as close to your mouth as possible.   Cover the mic if you know you are prone to plosive "p" sounds! If you don't have anything else your phone is probably better than your laptop because it's a phone, and so is designed to capture sound. Use a small room with lots of furniture and absorbent materials, big curtains are great. If you like, make your own sound booth by chucking a jacket or dressing gown over your head! You can record you narration line by line into a piece of software like audacity, or paragraph by paragraph, then you can export it as a continuous sound file. Listen back to the first line or a test sentence and make sure that the sound quality is good enough. Speak in an animated way, use big hand gestures to help you know when to put emphasis on words. (You can record this as a piece to camera if you'd like your face on screen. This is more suitable for certain subjects.) Talk as if you are explaining this to one friend. Imagine that you want that friend to think it's the coolest most interesting thing they've ever heard of! If it helps, drag a friend in to listen to you explain!*

30 minutes. *Draw under a camera, make diagrams, PowerPoint slides, make titles in your video editing app. Draw or write on a tablet or iPad and capture the screen. Whatever you feel is the best way for you and your topic and your video to make attractive and engaging visuals. Don't worry about the video taking the same time as your voice over you can speed it up or slow it down in the editing software.*

40 minutes. *Compile your video in the editing software. Make the drawings or diagrams last as long as you are talking about them by changing their duration or playback speed or by clipping them. Emphasise big important points using big important text on the screen.*

20 minutes. *Check the level of the sound, is it loud enough? Apply compression if your editor has that function. Add some backing music if you think it suits and is not too distracting. Export your video and upload it to YouTube.*

2d. Categories of video

Grow your channel by catering for your audience.

Aside from teaching different things, your videos all have different purposes in terms of growing your channel and catering for your audience. And remember that these are not two different things.

Please your audience and it will grow in numbers.

Try to think of your videos in groups. Aim each group to do one of these three different things: *One to build subscribers. One to get views from existing subscribers. One for engagement from current fans.*

These are essentially the three categories of video.

Videos to build subscribers will have a researched and search engine optimised (SEO) title and meta data. You should pick titles which you know have a high chance of being found through your audience entering search terms. These videos should show your channel at its best, giving a description of the value proposition of the channel, and then delivering that value. Include a strong call to action to subscribe at the start and at the end of the video.

Videos to get views from existing subscribers will be videos that you know are tried and tested to be popular on your channel. Use the same themes, similar titles and styles of videos that you know will be popular with your audience.

Videos for engagement from your current fans aim to give value to the most engaged people on your channel. Think about the people who comment and engage with your videos and try to give them something that they want. Don't worry if this type of video doesn't achieve massive audiences, just try and understand, and speak directly to, your *fans*. Use these to build community around your purpose.

A good content strategy will include a mixture of these three categories of video. You can change the relative numbers of each as your audience grows and you understand what they want more. I'm going to go into a little more detail about this in the chapter understanding "discoverability online".

Whether your content aims to be inspirational, or to deliver new learning, or revision. Whether you are going through exam technique or giving study tips. It will help you to think of your videos in these broad categories as they link very firmly to the way in which content gets discovered on YouTube.

Searchable videos for discovery (SEO).

These are the easiest way to get views when just starting.

AQA GCSE Physics - Paper 1 - memorise these - the night before the exam
30K views • Streamed 1 year ago

GorillaPhysics - Grade 9 and A* Physics

Here's a summary all the bits you need to have ready to go for AQA GCSE Physics Paper 1 on Wednesday. Here are some useful ...

Suggested videos which appear alongside other videos or in homepage feeds.

This is easiest to get views once you have a YouTube presence.

How to Study Effectively for Exams - tips to get the most out of revision time
1K views • 8 months ago

GorillaPhysics - Grade 9 and A* Physics

This is how to study for exams. Don't waste your time with poor revision techniques! I give you the best tips on how to maximise ...

Hero videos for returning viewers or direct from website or app, these can deliver a well thought out controlled message.

These are easiest to get views to if you have another large online presence.

You are more than just a grade!
3.8K views • 1 year ago

GorillaPhysics - Grade 9 and A* Physics

Here's a story about a student that felt that at school they were considered as just a grade. I promise your teachers and the SLT at ...

Building a content strategy for growth.

A good content strategy will have a mixture of these categories of videos, and so will maximise both the opportunities of your channel to get discovered and to please the returning viewers as well. The more watch time you get, the more likely you are to get recommended by YouTube and appear higher in search.

In the examples of my own videos in each of the three categories hopefully you can see that the titles thumbnails and description all contribute to *getting the click*. They should be designed together and make sense as a whole.

Also you can see that the thumbnail suits the category, for example the video aimed at returning viewers features my face, hoping that they will think, *I like that guy's chat* and want to hear what I have to say for motivation.

Another contributing factor to the success of these videos is that the titles, thumbnail and first lines of the description all sit with my underpinning value proposition; my promise to teach them how to get the highest grades.

There is more on content strategy and how to get discovered in the chapters "YouTube Strategy" and "Understanding Discoverability Online".

There is one more person that you should be sure to make videos for; *yourself!* Otherwise you will experience burn out! Make sure you enjoy making your videos, so that you can stay motivated.

Activity: Plan a series of videos for your channel using the three types of videos from the previous chapter and the three categories from this chapter. Design the titles and thumbnails first, and then plan the content of the videos to meet the expectations created by the title and thumbnail of each video.

Make it a short list of around 12 videos, with around; 6 tutorials, 4 exam technique videos, one study skills video and one video just about something that interests you.

Try to publish each on a Monday evening.

Evaluate the schedule in terms of how easy it was to stick to and whether you were happy with the results. Then write a schedule for the following three months.

2e. Structure of a video

The standard YouTube video structure:

Hook - reason to stick around through the video

Content

Call to action - reason to stay on your channel

It's easy to be sceptical of the standard YouTube structure. You can say *it's a formula!* And you'd be right. But it's an incredibly successful formula and many people enjoy it and consume hours and hours of content each day. For people under 35, on average, more than they watch TV.

Besides, knowing that you should start your video with a hook is not the same as being able to start a video with an *effective* hook.

Knowing that it is best practice to tell your viewers to subscribe and turn on notifications is not the same as actually having the gumption to go ahead and say it in the video, or to make it seem natural and not needy or desperate! The call to action is something I'm still developing; I find it hard to make it work naturally in my content. I've settled for a silent title at the end of the videos like *subscribe for more* or *hit the like button*. But these are nowhere near as compelling as the natural way that most successful YouTube creators deliver their subscribe call to actions.

Enjoy playing about with your YouTube structure. There is no absolute correct video structure. However, it is true that viewers have certain expectations when watching a YouTube video, and it is worth getting to know these conventions before you break them!

Foremost do not waste their time!

For educational content a good rule of thumb is to start delivering value straight away. Ideally you want to cut every distraction if it's at all likely be to result in them clicking away.

A common YouTube mistake is to start with a long intro. Long intros do not make your channel look more professional or more appealing. Viewers on YouTube expect to be engaged straight away. Anything which detracts from that will lead them to be questioning if any of the other suggested videos that YouTube is presenting to them will be more likely to answer their query and give them the value that they are after.

This table below summarises what the most common structure of videos on YouTube is. I would recommend that as you begin to make videos that you use this structure. Later as you develop you can enjoy experimenting, and reacting to the trends you notice about the way viewers do or do not engage with the videos.

6 seconds. Confirm the value promised by the title.	6 seconds. Very short intro and subscribe cue.	As long as you need. Content of the video.	20 seconds. Call to action and handoff to next video.
Get straight to the point. Start delivering the value straight away.	Whole channel message or tag line. Tell them why they should subscribe.	Give the audience what you promised. Make it as concise as possible. Deliver clearly and with appropriate pace. Chop it into discrete sections if it makes sense, consider chopping into separate videos if it gets too long.	Tell them what they should do next. Point them to your other videos, or tell them to go to a website, or tell them to subscribe, (or to buy your book!)

A more complex structure.

Importantly the video needs to start immediately delivering content. The viewer's confidence in you will grow as they watch more. But you need their very first impression of you to be that they are confident in your ability to teach them what they wanted to be taught.

Watch other channels and take ideas but try to settle on a structure that you like and that you feel will keep people watching and likely to come back for more later.

Look closely at videos on YouTube and you'll notice that the more prolific and expert YouTubers are adapting their video structure to fit the story that they are trying to tell. They are great at dropping in; call-to-action reads, deeper meaning or *thing under the thing* statements, and even promotions; in ways that you don't notice. It just feels normal to have told you to go subscribe, or to buy their stuff! But they won't do that if it doesn't suit the "category" or the tone of the video that they are making. A confident YouTuber makes it look like they don't plan the structure of the video, and the placement of the *video elements* (like subscribe calls to action). In reality they plan them very carefully.

Below is a video structure that I've been using recently to plan my videos. I've tried to think of all of the possible elements that I could work into a good video, and then bring them in when it feels right in the video. Or to just leave them out if they are not right for that video.

Some of the elements that I have not talked about yet are, the *Hook - Outcome – Testimonial* start of the video. This essentially means, tell them *why they should watch, what they will get by watching, and how they know it will work.*

You will see a box for the auto play visual hook. This is because in the YouTube app on mobile the video will start to play silently in the video feed. Having the first few seconds being very visually appealing is a good way to attract attention to your video.

There's a box for the call to action with a value statement, (because I need to train myself to say it every time!)

There are lots of self-explanatory curriculum type boxes and one box for the outline. There's one for key diagrams that I need to include.

Then for the outro, you'll see a box to remind me to ask them to engage with the video by either liking or commenting on the video. There is an idea to get viewers to do something which is very easy to do, for example just to comment *boom* in the comments section.

Thumb	Title	
SEO	Hook - Outcome – Testimonial H - Deliver the value promised in the title. O - I'm going to show you how to master the questions on ….....	First 30s (auto play visual hook)
Tags	T - other channels cover the content but GorillaPhysics will get you the grade 9/A*	Context
Curriculum Point	Intro C2A If you want to get the highest grades in your Physics qualifications, GorillaPhysics has the highest-level videos to get you the grade 9 or A* Subscribe and ring the bell. I've got lots of other study related stuff too. Plus lower third C2A later in video	
	Explanation	Demos
Repetitive key point		Images
Example Questions/ What you have to do with this in the exam		Diagrams
		Hard Bits
	Video Description	
Playlist	Middle Engagement - simple comment "boom" if this explanation makes sense	Watch this next…
		Likes
	Outro (engagement) more questions on this? GorillaPhysics.com	

2f. Developing your style

Is it better than the 1920s?

In some of my recent videos I have used public domain footage from the first half of the 20th century. I even used one silent film, complete with dialogue sides from silent movies of the time!

But they are really very good! They have actual demonstrations of the physics that they are teaching. They have stop motion and light drawing animations of electrons being made to move in the wire. They have very carefully thought about the best way to explain what they are trying to teach.

They haven't just rolled the camera as they talk over a chalk board or made some scruffy hand drawn diagrams on a piece of paper to make their point.

My point I'd like to make is that your videos need to be an improvement on what is already out there. Otherwise, why should you bother making them?

I think that you *should* bother making new videos to explain your topics, or to help young people in their academic journey, or whatever type of content that you see yourself making. But you have to commit to developing a style which is yours, and which is better than, or different to, what already exists.

You need to figure out what you are offering and why your video should be watched *rather* than what already exists. You need to find your own unique selling point, your USP.

The internet has a lot of explanations of every part of every syllabus that we teach. But we do not have *your* explanation! Give it with confidence but make it something special, create something which adds value to what exists in your area.

Is it like having a textbook read to you?

One of my favourite YouTube channels is *Minute Physics*. When I was starting out making YouTube videos, I watched a lot of videos by channels that I admired that were on the subject of making videos. Henry Reich, the creator of *Minute Physics'* short form, hand drawn, animated videos talks about his videos offering more than what you can get from a textbook.

He compares his videos to other educational videos, which typically are longer chats through a topic, as the teacher writes on the screen and monotonously reads through the explanation that they have prepared. There's nothing wrong with this he says, but *it feels like having a textbook read to you. Which, why would you want that, when you could just pick up a textbook and read it.*

On the one hand your videos being compared to a textbook could be seen as a very good thing. Textbooks are brilliant, they are meticulously researched, carefully written and accurate explanations. They have great value. But Henry wants his videos to be more than that. His drawings engage the viewer as he leads them through the core elements of a topic in a well written, well presented exploration of the wonderment of an area of physics. He hopes to spark your interest such that you be inspired to pick up that weighty volume and read to find the details of the subject matter.

Reading is still the most effective and efficient way to record and communicate ideas. I think that there is something about the way our mind works around *written words* which cannot be replicated in any other medium. We can all construct different meanings as we read the same text and these unique meanings get applied to our own context giving unique value.

This is a very different experience to watching a video, perhaps because videos are temporal and linear. They have an exact message, which closes off further thought around the idea. I, for example, get some of my best ideas when reading. I am constantly using the parts of my brain not mechanically scanning the words to think of how I can use the ideas that the writer is giving to me.

The converse of Henry's short, snappy, scripted and wonderful video style is the *Khan Academy* style. Sal Khan believes that videos should be conversational in tone, relaxed, repeating key points and not being afraid to elaborate for understanding. The *Khan Academy* presenters carry the viewers through the video on a wave of personable, confident and friendly narration.

However, both Henry and Sal talk about their videos being, *like you're sat next to them, talking them through the topic.* Both have developed an engaging style. Neither is better, but they are both watchable, and that is the important thing!

Find yourself on video.

Whether you are appearing on video or narrating over images that you draw or present you need to find your own style as a presenter. If it is the first time you've appeared on video, you will probably find it quite unnatural talking to a camera. Often in your first videos your explanations will be slow and laborious.

To keep your audience engaged you must present with pace, clarity and personality. You probably have all three, you just need to find them in front of the camera. The way to do this is to find a way to relax.

Take the time to find yourself on camera. Remember it is not the same as talking to a class, if you don't get it right immediately it doesn't mean you can't do it!

My pro-tip here is to imagine that you are talking to just one of your students. One who listens attentively. I'm not saying your favourite student, (because they are all our favourites!) You know the one though, the one that sits at the front of the class and nods along.

I often film with a note behind the camera which says *calm down and be yourself.* If I feel myself getting wound up, or I feel that I'm not explaining with pace, clarity and personality, I just stop. Give myself a moment, think about what I'm saying, let myself calm down and then start again.

I also make a conscious decision when to film and when not to. I film when I'm feeling good and calm and I'm not self-conscious, or worried about anything else which might be going on in my work or personal life.

Remember it's natural to be nervous in front of the camera, nerves just show you care.

To script or not to script?

Let's go back to the comparison I made between *Minute Physics* videos and *Khan Academy* videos. One is completely scripted out, and the other intentionally unscripted. There are pros and cons of both methods of figuring out what will be said on a video, both can lead to really engaging narration, but they take different skill sets to get right. If your skills lend themselves to writing, perhaps scripting your videos is a better plan. If your skills lend themselves to confidently thinking on your feet, or you know you have the *gift of the gab,* then probably you'll be better suited to ad lib your way through the topics, (provided you know them really well and your video outlines are well planned.)

When you are new to it, you might want to write scripts word for word to avoid sounding nervous. Then as you gain confidence, you'll naturally find that you adapt from your script as you talk, so that the video feels more natural. Then eventually you can freestyle the bits that you are most confident with.

I have never fully scripted any of my videos, but I have scripted some bits (important bits) word for word. I use scripting when I get a certain idea that I want to convey in exactly the way the idea came to me. Other bits need to be more natural. Especially if I'm filming something that I'm really confident with, or perhaps something that I've just taught to a class, or given an assembly on, I feel well-rehearsed and that I can just press record and feel confident about getting the sequence right, and delivering with pace, clarity and personality.

If I'm honest this has not been the best policy, as I am certainly not as confident on camera as I would like to be, (or as I would like to think I am!) If I had scripted my early videos, they would be better quality than they are. I would recommend anyone who is just starting making educational videos to script their videos in their entirety.

For me whether I choose to script or not comes down to a choice as to where I would prefer to spend my time. Scripting takes time before filming to think carefully about how to say something. But it usually means that the editing process is a little more streamlined, because you are essentially just selecting the best take and using that. Not scripting takes less time before filming. Perhaps you just work off a set of bullet points. As it involves sometimes saying the wrong things, or changing your mind while filming, it means editing takes longer as you need to select the best narration during the editing process.

If you are going for fully scripted videos, I suggest that you try using voice recognition software, or the dictate feature in word to write them. This should mean that your script has a natural spoken word flow to it. It will also speed up your script writing process!

Once you've done the a few times, you might feel that you might as well have recorded your narration as you wrote it!

There is one more benefit to scripting your videos that I haven't discussed yet, and this is closed captions. Closed captions, i.e. subtitles, can be entered into YouTube line by line as the speaker talks. These are translated by Google Translate into every language that it can, and so your video has the potential to be consumed in more countries. It also helps the YouTube search engine indexing bots to know more about the content of the video and so present that video more accurately in search.

By default, YouTube listens to your video and makes a set of closed captions, but these are not always perfectly accurate. This is especially a problem if your subject material is very specialised, which it tends to be on education channels.

If you have the videos scripted exactly you can quickly copy and paste the script into the closed captions dialogue. This will ensure accuracy and so better search engine optimisation and more accurate translations.

There are services that you can pay for that will enter closed captions for you. Check out *rev.com* for one example of a company that will subtitle your videos for around a pound per minute.

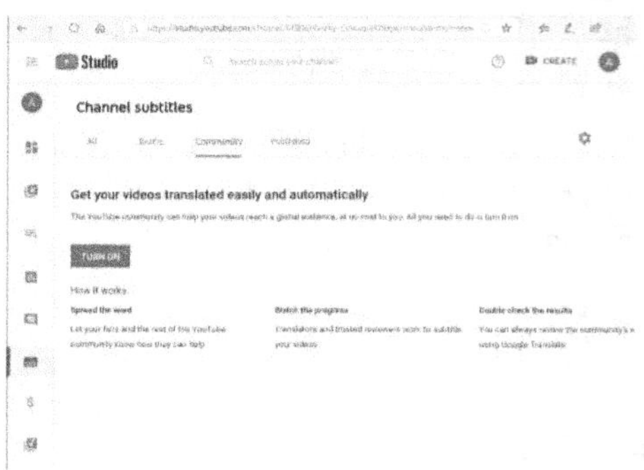

It's also possible to ask your viewers, or fans, or a friend or neighbour, to do it for you. All you need to do is enable community subtitles and anyone can add captions. And you retain the rights to finally publish or delete them.

Activity: If you usually script then try unscripted, if you usually go unscripted then try a script! Pick a straightforward topic that you would find easy to explain in your class for this task, so it doesn't take long; because this task is all in a the evaluation. Did it take less time working in the other way? Is it clearer? Does your personality come through stronger? Do you get better feedback in the comments, or from your class? Does it perform better over time?

Engage your audience.

The key to engaging your audience is to know them. Do your research. And spend time during your planning of your videos thinking about how the typical member of your audience will receive your video and engage with it.

We considered questions like these in the chapter "This Book" and we'll consider them again in the chapter "Growing Your Audience". They are questions which will help you sculpt videos which truly matter to your audience and should be revisited time and time again.

Start your research with the competition. There's plenty of room for everyone on YouTube, but whether you like it or not, as an education channel you will always be competing with other channels for the viewers to choose your videos!

What teacher YouTube channels exist already for your subject?

How are you going to be better than them?

If you cannot be better than them, how are you going to be different to them?

Different may in fact be more likely to lead to success than trying to be better than them at something that they are more established at and have been doing for some time.

Then research your audience.

What ages are they?

What other interests do they have?

What decisions are they likely to make about the educational content that they consume?

Importantly, what level are you aiming at?

Consider whether you are going to target the very engaged students, who like depth, breadth and challenge. Or whether you are looking to provide low commitment and high value content to students who just want the quickest way to *pass* maths GCSE, for example.

To reach your target audience you are going to have to beat the competition. You need to make a small percentage of the people studying your subject trust you more than they trust the other channels offering to teach the same content.

Activity: Write a value statement for your channel. Make it a sort of slogan that you want people to associate with your channel. Try and sum up the reason why people should watch your videos on your topics rather than any other.

Try out a few short value statements in your next few videos you create. Test out how they sound coming out of your mouth. Make sure that you are comfortable saying them and they accurately convey the value you are offering to your viewers.

Alternative structures of explanations and lengths of videos.

There are many ways to start an explanation. Consider whether other ways to structure your explanations could be more engaging than just starting delivering information from the first word in the video.

Perhaps try starting with a problem and offering a solution. Perhaps try videos which challenge misconceptions. Or try explanations which start in a context. Perhaps try explaining how something works, or why something is the way it us.

Experiment, enjoy it, and reflect on what hits a note with your audience.

Education videos are not entertainment, but you do need to hold interest. Remember you do not have a captive audience, like in a lesson or at a lecture. And you don't have immediate feedback to work off!

In the chapter "Analytics: which bits matter? And what does it all mean?" I'll discuss the valuable feedback that you can get about your videos by analysing your audience retention graphs. These graphs show that they *can and will leave.* Luckily though, in analysing these graphs you can get a good idea about what makes them likely to stay, or to leave.

You will not get this right every time, I certainly haven't! But you'll learn as you go on. Think of ways that *you* can keep attention.

Don't be ashamed to use some of the tricks of TV, or of YouTube, to keep engagement.

Throw forward to the next videos. Think carefully about the big value of the video and tell them to make sure they stay to the end to find out. Tell them why your video is valuable and what they will get from it.

Build rituals that are natural to you and your audience, for example if it makes sense to you and your channel, tell repeated *in-jokes,* so that they are watching, waiting for you to make the next joke.

And discover your teacher personality on camera. Just remember it might have to be different to your personality in the classroom!

2g. Engagement matters

Carry them with you.

The hardest thing to master is keeping people engaged. This is true on video as well as in the classroom. When I am recording or editing my videos, I am always thinking about carrying the audience with me through an explanation. I need to tread this fine line between explaining every point thoroughly and moving on quickly enough such that my viewers aren't getting bored.

When I first started making videos, I imagined myself being the same animated and engaging speaker on video that I was in front of my classes. I was immediately aware that this wasn't easy.

Like a performer, the teacher in the classroom uses the feedback of the class to know when they are going too slow, or too fast. They gauge whether the class are bored and can interject an interesting example or anecdote into their lesson. They can tell by the looks on the faces, and by using questions whether they need to go other something again.

With video therefore you need to approach your planning in a different way. You can't just turn up and riff, as many great teachers are capable of doing in their classrooms. You need to plan for a silent classroom. Think about where you are likely to lose the lower ability viewers and where you will bore those with greater confidence in the material.

One way to overcome the challenge of lack of feedback is to ensure that the level of the video is advertised. Make it clear if the video is aimed at higher of foundation students. Explain whether this is a video summarising and revising a large topic, and viewers should be familiar with the ideas already, or is a video proposing to teach everything from scratch, perhaps with exercises for the students to complete.

Another way to approach this engagement is to employ the vehicle of storytelling. This is easy to do in topics where there is a literal and established story to be related. *The development of the model of the atom* is one which springs to mind in physics; the ideas of people challenging accepted ideas is an easy one to engage your audience with.

But storytelling is harder to do in more obscure topics, or perhaps exam skills or study tip videos. Perhaps the story then is more about the person looking for the guidance that your video proposes to offer. Perhaps the story is about a student that was struggling with their revision, *just like the viewer*. And your video is about your experience of how students like that overcome their difficulties.

Simple stories have three main elements; *desire, conflict and resolution.*

Desire	Conflict	Resolution
A character has something that they want.	There are obstacles that they need to overcome to get what they want.	In overcoming the obstacles, they learn something or grow as a person.

Think of any story that you love, and you will probably be able to summarise the plot in this standard, three-act structure.

This is not to say that it is a great idea to over emphasise the three-act structure, but to subtly weave a story into your content is a great way to get engagement. And, if you can hold your audience through the majority of your videos, YouTube will promote your videos and your channel will grow rapidly.

Here's an example of what the three-act structure might look like for an exam solution video:

Desire	Conflict	Resolution
Students often struggle with this type of question.	It's hard because of this tricky skill that you've got to master in order to get it right.	As long as you practice this skill, you can now avoid this mistake in your exams.

Here's an example of what the three-act structure might look like for a topic tutorial lesson:

Desire	Conflict	Resolution
My class always find this topic hard.	They struggle with the concept that change x causes change y.	But as soon as they know the key points by heart, they end up understanding it well.

Good narratives are the gold standard of creating videos, you should aspire to do it well. It might not feel natural at first, but it is a sure way to increase engagement. The audience will stay to watch more of a well-structured story, and they will be more likely to make a visible *engagement*.

Engagements, i.e. comments, likes, subscribes and shares, all tell YouTube that people like your video and they will recommend it more.

But the most important reason they will recommend your video is if people watch the majority of it. Never lose sight of this as you make your videos. YouTube wants to keep people watching for longer. The more you do this the more the algorithm will put your video in front of people.

How long should it be?

Conventional wisdom is that the shorter the video is, the better. A more likely answer though is; *as long as it should be for that type of video, for that category of video and for that topic of video.*

For example; I might make a longer video if it were aimed at my returning viewers, my core audience, and make a shorter video if it were a video aimed at getting views from search and winning subscribers to my channel.

If you want a time to aim for when your channel is young, many would say that the target average watch time to be best picked up by the algorithm, is four minutes. And, you need to have 50% average viewing percentage for your videos to be regularly recommended, so that would point to eight minutes being the ideal YouTube video length. For me, the only rule about how long a video should be is; *no longer than it needs to be.*

The often-overlooked cue to click on a particular video, which is shown in the bottom right corner of the thumbnail, is the video length. This, along with the thumbnail, title and first lines of the description, make up all that your viewers will have to go on to decide which video to choose to answer their query.

Consider which clip you would click when you want to know something specific, 3 mins or 15mins? Probably the 3 minutes. But then consider, if you are sitting down to a study session and your search query was something like, *GCSE Romeo and Juliet revision*, perhaps you would pick the 15 minute video over the 3 minute as you'd be confident that they were going to cover more depth.

Just remember not to waste time. If you start the 15 minute video and they ramble for the first 30 seconds, you'll probably go back to the 3 minute video! Don't be repetitive, people can rewind if they want to recap something you said.

And the worst thing for your video is if people leave it all at the same point because you seem to be saying the same thing you've already said twice before!

It's really common to plan a video out and imagine it taking only two minutes to explain! Then once you're done talking you have a thirty-minute video! Think about how many lessons it takes to teach that topic in the classroom. You can think about your videos one objective at a time. And if you do find yourself taking much longer than expected, you can always chunk it down into separate videos in the editing process. You can then organise your videos in playlists for longer viewing sessions.

As a viewer I use the time stamp in different ways depending on the purpose of my view. If I'm choosing a video to entertain me, I'll go for a length which best fits the time I have available for that casual viewing session. If I'm picking a video to learn something though, all other things being equal, I'll pick the video which offers the same value in the shortest time.

Comments and community.

I've had very few negative comments on my channel in the six years I've been making videos. I've had still fewer abusive comments.

I've had thousands of positive comments. And most importantly I've had comments which have made my day, when I've been having a difficult one!

I'd encourage you not to be frightened of the comment section. See as the place in which you build community, and from that community you build engagement.

Match the content, to the purpose of your audience, and you will not fail to build a community. Initially it might be centred around a small group of people that you know in real life, perhaps your own class and school. But later you'll have so many more viewers.

Be confident to share your videos, but don't do it in a spammy way. If the quality is there, people will watch, and people will share your videos. Think carefully about when and where people are likely to find your videos and go meet them on those platforms and share your videos there!

Do not get disheartened! If you title videos right, if you teach well in them, your videos will find an audience.

I'll talk more about how your videos will be found by an audience in the chapter "Understanding discoverability online."

2h. Technical stuff (gear)

Principles of "good enough" production value.

For education channels the gear doesn't matter. But there's a minimum production quality which you must meet in order for your videos to be watchable. In other words; if you don't get a few simple things right, viewers will not stick around to watch your content.

The principles you'll meet in the chapter "Technical stuff (shooting)" are; *light, camera* and *sound*. That means; plenty of light, falling on your face or whatever you are filming, a well composed, steady (locked-off) camera shot, and clear, loud, audible sound.

The minimum gear you need for this is a window and a smartphone. You can get plenty of diffuse light providing you can film in the day with a large enough window behind the camera. You can lock your phone off with a few well-placed books, and the camera in your smartphone is likely to be good enough. The microphones in smartphones are pretty good, (because they are phones, so they have to record clear audio,) and they will sound ok providing you are close enough and not in an echoey room.

Expensive gear therefore is completely unnecessary, but it does make it easier to achieve the three important things to get right when shooting video. I recommend, if you have nothing else, just to start filming with nothing but your phone. Enjoy it, get used to being on camera and learn the craft of making a good YouTube video!

That being said, as you begin to make more videos, pay attention to the things that are not as good as they could be. Compare your videos with other videos on YouTube and ask yourself what technical aspects you want to improve. A small outlay can drastically improve the technical quality of your videos. If you are serious about your YouTube channel, then it is normal and the right thing to want to produce the very best videos that you can.

The content of your videos will always beat the technical quality of your videos, providing the production value is "good enough". But it's a much greater joy to make videos that you are proud to share with the world. Besides, gear is fun!

I'm going to talk you through three set-ups one around £100, one around £500 and one £1000 or more. The great thing about gear is that you can start cheap, and then just keep adding gear as and when you feel that you need to upgrade.

Around £100

Adding an external lavalier microphone allows the mic to be as close as possible to your mouth. These are the ones that you'll see clipped onto presenters' ties, or lapels or collars on TV. It just picks up sound from the immediate vicinity, so will not be as affected by a noisy environment. The *Rode Smartlav +* is an inexpensive microphone which plugs straight into a headphone jack on a phone, (or by adapter with the latest *iPhones* and *Android* devices). I recommend it as the first thing you buy to improve the quality of your videos.

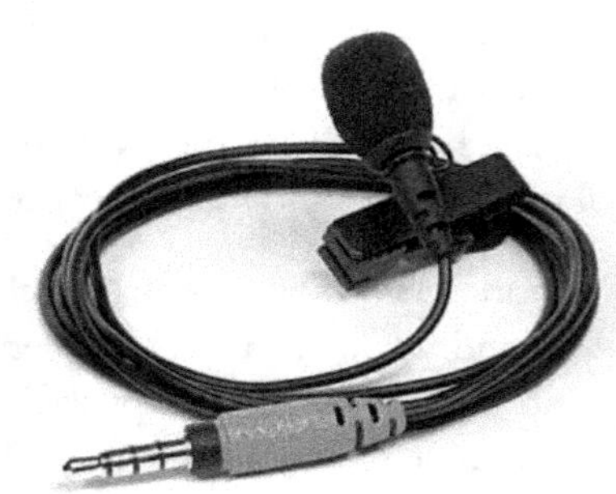

https://amzn.to/2CsXv6v

Other steps you can take to improve sound for absolutely nothing is just to pick a room which has no bare walls. Rooms with books on shelves, large curtains, or notice boards all act to absorb sound rather than reflect it, and this leads to clearer sound.

Something like this *Joby Gorillapod* for smartphones, or really any small, cheap phone tripod can make it much easier to set up the shots that you want. Look for one with a ball head, and that allows you to have as much versatility as possible.

https://amzn.to/3kvq1FI

I also quite like the cheaper grip style mini tripods such as these. They are compact and are easy to set up.

https://amzn.to/399T2Sl

Use the main (rear) camera on your phone as this is likely to be a better quality than the front facing "selfie" camera.

If you cannot always film during the day, near a big window then investing in lighting is the best thing that you can do. Simple LED lights can be very cheap and upgrade the look of your footage massively. Here's

an example of a ring light that comes with its own stand. Make sure lighting is above your face and the camera for a natural look. Look for lights which are rechargeable or USB powered, and think about what will fit in with your space that you'll be filming in.

https://amzn.to/3alGbgB

Ring lights are intended for beauty videos more than educational videos, but they give a pleasing natural light on faces and reduce harsh shadows. If you can mount them downwards around a visualiser it will also help prevent harsh shadows on your work.

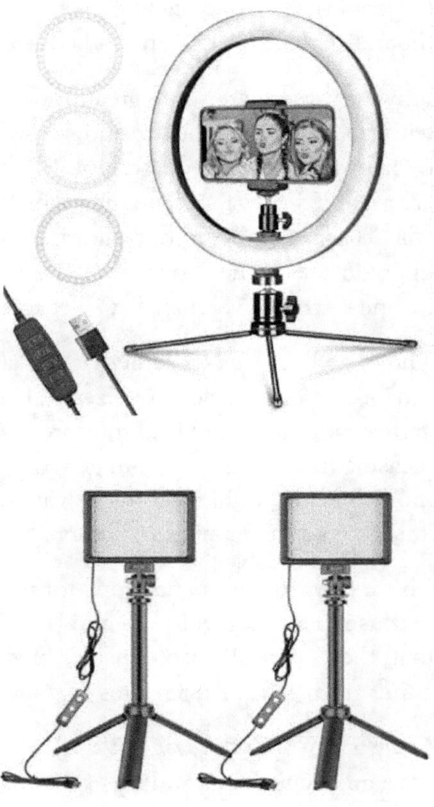

These inexpensive LED panel lights are also a great option, which will enable you to have lights in multiple places and organise your lighting in various creative ways. They can be dimmed so that one can be your bright key light and another your dimmer fill light.

https://amzn.to/3li0LTS

LED lights can stay with you as you upgrade your set up. A professional studio set-up will have many lights. A cheap LED light that you buy when you are getting started can be a background or a fill light when you progress to the next level of set-up.

Around £500.

The most expensive part of most studios is the camera system. Camera bodies and camera lenses can run into the thousands. At this level we are going to stick to the consumer level of cameras, but any of the choices below will be a major upgrade on any smartphone camera.

I would recommend an interchangeable lens system camera, as this will allow you to upgrade in the future. Lenses are typically more expensive than the camera bodies, as typically the lens makes a bigger difference to the quality of the image than the camera body does.

However, there are some great options with fixed lenses if you are sure that you'll be happy with the standard look. They are great if you want something which will do a great job and not want to upgrade later. Check out the *Canon G7X* or one of the newer *Sony RX100* cameras.

The benefit of a *proper* camera is the larger sensor and optical element sizes. These gather more light and lead to more pleasing images. They are in general more versatile and lead to more variation in shot type than a phone camera.

I have some recommendations for great starter camera kits. I won't post links because the prices will vary, and you should look for the camera for cheaper than the list price! Also consider buying one of these cameras second hand either from *eBay* or from sites like *mpb.com*.

Canon EOS M50 or *canon 250d* have great autofocus and a massive range of lenses. They are light and small and very easy to use. Grab an extra lens like the *EF-S 10-18mm* for wide shots or one of the many inexpensive canon prime lenses that you'll find out there for some attractive looking depth of field effects.

The *Sony 6000* series of cameras are an incredibly versatile set of cameras. Sony currently make the most technically impressive cameras that you can buy. They are probably the cameras to go for if you feel that you are likely to get interested in what higher technical specifications of cameras can do for your videos.

The *Panasonic G80,* and the other cameras in the G-mount micro four thirds system are also worth a look. They offer great feature sets in compact, lightweight form factors. There is a great range of lenses and an excellent feature set. These are probably the all-round use option! I personally use a *GX8* which meets my needs very well.

Do some research and decide which system is right for you. But before you buy check what you already own, or what might be gathering dust in a relative's cupboard. Any digital camera bought in the last decade it probably shoots full HD video, this is good enough for YouTube.

Make sure any camera you buy has a microphone input, and all the features you think you'll need.

HD video is a minimum. High resolution 4K is a nice to have but not necessary for all but some specialised use cases.

Make sure the camera and lens have the option for a nice wide angle shot, especially if you'll be filming in a small space, or if you want to carry it around and "vlog" with it. Look at what lenses are available on the system and consider whether you'll be able to afford to upgrade lenses later on should you wish.

Lastly a screen which can flip to be visible from the front is almost essential for YouTube because most of us film on our own, and it makes it so much easier to compose the shot! Just make sure to look down the lens rather than check yourself out in the screen as you speak!

A *proper* camera requires a *proper* tripod! There are two options, an inexpensive full tripod is the most useful for being able to compose and shot. But they are big and cumbersome. If you think you'll always shoot in the same place and can leave this set up, go for this option. I recommend this *Neewer* tripod to most people in education because of the option to give you the *top down shot* with your higher quality camera.

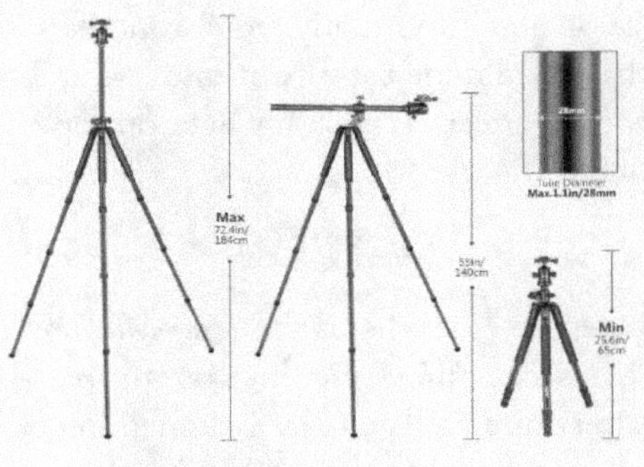

https://amzn.to/2F8FCuT

A table-top tripod allows far more options than the smaller *gorillapod* type tripod but is far easier thing to set up and break down and carry around than a full-size tripod. Go for this option if you think you'll be filming in various places or carrying gear around with you regularly. Small tripods can also be great advantages for handheld video. Aside from having more ways to grip your camera, having weight under the camera can act like a steady cam and remove some of the jittery motion you get when hand holding cameras. I own both of these tripods I mention, and I use the table-top tripod more often!

https://amzn.to/2F7ElUW

Shot gun mics are not always an improvement over lav mics, but it is really easy to get good quality sound with a shot gun mic. They are directional, so they pick up sound from sources that they are pointed at rather than all around.

Rode are one of the most popular microphone brands and this is because they are both inexpensive and high quality. There are other inexpensive brands worth checking out, for example *BOYA* and *Deity*, however neither have the long-term reputation for both quality and value that *Rode* has.

You can start with the *VideoMicro Compact On Camera Microphone*. This is a least expensive option and importantly requires no batteries. I have had mine for 5 years and it is still working great. It basically lives on top of my camera.

https://amzn.to/2F8GwaL

A step up from that is the *VideoMic Pro Compact Directional On Camera Microphone*. This is three times the price but probably not three times the quality. It also is battery operated so there is something else to remember to keep charged, but it will give you clearer sound and be less susceptible to "clipping" which is when a sound is too loud to register on the mic and just becomes a fuzzy bunch of loud clicks and makes the audio basically unusable.

https://amzn.to/3fDzhnD

Third option from *Rode* is the *Wireless Go – Compact Wireless Microphone System.*
This is a wireless lav mic, including a USB rechargeable transmitter with a built-
in high-quality microphone, or a stereo
jack for any other microphone you
would wish to use mounted away from
your camera. It is a brilliant system at
a very high value price and is definitely
the option if you are going to be
moving around a lot in your videos at
any distance from the camera.

https://amzn.to/2XHFEAe

Microphones aren't cool or aspirational to use in the way that an amazing
camera or lens is, but they do more for the quality and watchability of your final
product than anything else that you can invest your money in.

Similarly, if you are not happy with the way your videos look compared to other
people on YouTube you should certainly look to improve your lighting before
you blame it on the quality of your camera and lens. A poorly lit shot will still
look rubbish on an amazing camera!

As a rule, larger, brighter, more diffuse sources of light always improve video
quality. There are two main options, the cheaper is a set of studio video lights,
with large fluorescent bulbs and big "soft boxes", which are like big white tents.
You can get a pair or set of three of these for very little.

Here's the pair that I own, which I
like, and which would be great if I
had a studio space that I could just
leave them set up. In reality
because of their size and how
cumbersome they are to set up I
only really use them when I know I
will be doing a lot of filming that
day or week to come. If I did have
a dedicated studio space, I would
have four of these and just leave
them set up.

https://amzn.to/3ipDoFP

Larger panel LED lighting is cheaper than you might think. They take up a lot
less room than the soft box type of light! Another advantage is that they are

dimmable and you can also set the colour
temperature of the white light they produce.
Again, *Neewer* do the best balance between
quality and price. Here's a set of three LED
panels which would be a great studio set up
for very little outlay:

https://amzn.to/2PFjcmQ

The larger, wider, more diffuse sources give
fewer harsh shadows and will make things
look a lot nicer. I'll go into studio light set-
ups below but simply put the way to light a
person is to have a key light and a fill light. A key light is a bright light source
above and to one side of the subject, a fill light is a smaller dimmer light below
and to the opposite side from the key light. It reduces and softens shadows.

Other more creative looks can be achieved with RGB LED lights and panels,
where you can set the light to any colour you like. Also, there are a wide range
of higher quality options that you can look out for online. Have a little search
for LED video lights and you will find lots of good options. Some more
premium brands are *Aputure* and *Godox*. An alternative to get the coloured look
in your videos for less might be to look at the *Philips Hue* system of lights, which
aren't intended for video but will give you the same effect.

£1000 plus

You can spend thousands and thousands of pounds on cameras and lenses! and
I'm not going to list the best professional gear. But you can aspire to one day
filming on a full frame camera, shooting raw video in glorious 8K, and spending
the time making it look beautiful. These cameras are probably overkill for an
education YouTube channel, but if you are a large education brand and you
need to appear highly professional you'll find some great options here.

I recommend looking into the *Sony A7* line of cameras, or the cannon *EOS R*
mount cameras. Also, the more premium micro four thirds mount *Panasonic G9*
and *GH5* cameras are incredibly capable video cameras at reasonable prices.

In any more professional studio multiple camera set-ups or 4K cameras will
allow cutting to alternative angles or cropping and reframing during editing.
Remember though the higher spec the camera, and the more ambitious and
complex the editing, the more powerful the computer needs to be.

There are two uses for this technique, one is to hide cuts. The other is to bring focus onto something else in the video. I personally use this a lot in my videos. If I mess up my lines in a video I can cut, reframe the image and it looks as if I've cut for emphasis rather than to remove a section of video where I messed up some words or said a long *ummmm*....

I also often use second cameras to cover demonstrations or a close up of a white board. In which case I can cut to the close-up of the demo whilst still playing the audio of me talking throughout.

If you are buying for a large educational brand and want several people to be able to access and use the cameras, consider getting a set of the same model of cameras. This way all who sign out the cameras and use them will know the how to use them. You can also have a fleet of different lenses ready for the different types of videos you may wish to shoot for your brand.

Having multiple cameras can also allow you to shoot videos from multiple angles at the same time and this is one of the easiest ways to make your videos look professional. Switching framing and shots makes videos more visually appealing. For this reason, if you are making the choice between two "good enough" cameras or one more premium camera, I'd recommend the two.

A full tripod is a must in any pro set-up. Video tripods are use usually very large and heavy, this makes them very stable platforms, but unless you've invested in some serious cinema or TV camera, you'll get away with an inexpensive aluminium photography tripod. Video tripods also have fluid heads to allow them to do smooth pans, but again as you'll probably be on camera as well as operating the camera, you'll probably be happy just to use a tripod with a ball head.

Serious studio lights don't have to be massively expensive. But they do take up a lot of room. I own some lights with big soft boxes to give diffuse light over a large area, but I rarely set them up because the space I film in is so small! As such is recommend going with something that fits in your space rather than fits your aspirations as a film maker! LED panels are thinner and can give great effect and aren't necessarily overly expensive.

In the previous section I discussed the two most important lights for video, the fill and the key light. A more professional set-up would introduce (at least) two

more lights. The back light and
the backdrop light are
additional, creative lighting
choices that you can adjust to
your own tastes. They are
numbered in the diagram in
order of importance.

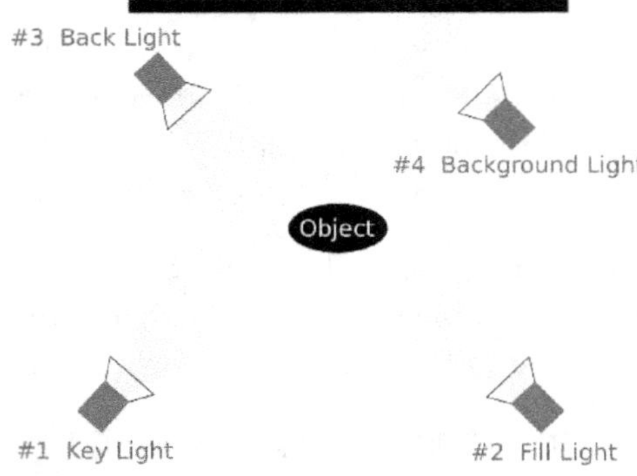

You would never film a person
without a key light. This is
usually a bright, diffuse light
source. Have it above the
person at around 45 degrees to look natural, (like the angle of the sun). The fill
light fills in harsh shadows. This is usually less bright, as you want some soft
shadows on a face for definition.

The back light, or sometimes called the "hair light" accents the outline of a
person's head, giving them great separation from the background and providing
a few highlights around the silhouette of the presenter. The background light
can eliminate any shadows created by the object on the backdrop. It can give
you a flat colour across the back, for example if you are going to be doing any
"green screen" (technically called "colour keying") effects. Otherwise, this
background lighting could be many lights, of any colour. Or you could choose
to have a very dark background, such that your subject is separated in that way.

Two additions to transform any room into a YouTube studio are backdrops
and sound proofing. Backdrops can be like large roller blinds which you can
pull down behind you to give your space a professional look, (and hide your
messy shelves!) Backdrops can also be useful if you wish to replace your
background. They don't have to be green, but this is the most used colour
because it's not often worn! Sound proofing, especially on the corners of the
room just cut out that echo leading to clearer more pleasing sound.

XLR mics are the industry standard way to power a mic. They have the largest
range of loudness that they record and so will avoid clipping, which is when a
sound is too loud for the microphone and you just get a click on the
soundtrack. You can avoid this by recording slightly quieter than you'd expect
the want your final video to be exported at. Most professional microphones
offer a way to vary the gain and use the mic level indicators on more
professional cameras to see that when you talk you are not getting near the
maximum loudness for that microphone. An alternative is to monitor the audio
whilst recording to keep checking that it sounds clear and doesn't click. This
isn't really possible when you are recording on your own though!

Absorbent materials, like curtains, or furniture coverings are all you really need to deaden the echoes in a room, but professional studios with large budgets will work in rooms with higher quality acoustic foam, sound proof boards on the walls, or purpose made absorbent blankets hung around their studio to get rid of any echoes and reverb which will make your audio less pleasing to hear.

Boom stands are another great way to improve your audio, so that the microphone can be just out of shot above your mouth. Mounting a shotgun mic pointing directly at the mouth just a few inches above the speaker is a common way to achieve this.   Remember the rule that the closer the microphone is to someone the better the voice is going to sound.

Setting up a studio space in an office if you are an educational brand is a great idea. Or if you are an individual, look to set up a studio in a home office, spare room or corner of your living room. Having a space which is always set up ready to use avoids the creative block of having to get gear out and set up rather than just being able to power on the lights and get started.

Activity: Design your own studio space! This can be anywhere! Many YouTube videos are filmed in a garage or the corner of a bedroom… and you'd never guess! If you have a large spare room that you can convert into a full time studio that is ideal. If you're a education business then you'll probably want to find a room in your office space to be a permanent studio.

Decide on where the camera is going to be, what's in the background of the shot and where you are going to sit or stand. Think about what you can place in the shot and what you can get rid of. Try and include objects which hint at your brand, your USP and your value proposition.

Try and keep things tidy because clutter can be very distracting, but it's easy to just clear out junk to behind the camera when you record! Try and have things in the shot that reflect what your channel is all about, for example I have a Newton's Cradle on my desk (and a gorilla.)

Once you've figured out the space have a think about what gear you'll need to make this a quality looking video and go back through the gear list and just order what you need. Focus especially on lighting, a tripod and a good microphone. Coloured background lighting can be especially pleasing to the eye.

Equipment for other types of video.

Webcams are great for recording images
of yourself while presenting, and as long
as you just want a small image of
yourself in one corner then they are
good enough quality. However, the
webcams built into most laptops, even
premium ones are usually pretty poor.
What is more is that you cannot place
them anywhere you like and so you
often get the really unflattering up the
nose, or double chin, camera angle. I
would strongly recommend buying a
USB webcam that you can place on a

tabletop tripod and set up the angle just as you like. The *Logitech C920 HD Pro
Webcam* is the most popular choice, once again, as it is the best balance between
quality and price.

https://amzn.to/3ad5eCd

There are ways to use your phone as a webcam linked to your computer or as a
visualiser, check out apps like *IPEVO's iDoc-Cam* or *droidCam* for ways to
wirelessly send your phone's camera image to your computer. However,
sometimes having the right gear is just about making your workflow straight
forward and making sure that you don't have any time or creativity wasted
setting stuff up!

If you plan on doing the top-down, talk through videos, a visualiser is essential.
Otherwise you can mount your camera, or a USB webcam, facing top down. I
find the *IPEVO VZ-X* or *VZ-R* to be great options as they have a HDMI

output and so can be used in the
classroom without needing to link to a
computer. However, if you are only
interested in recording videos to the
computer then you should get the
IPEVO DO-CAM. It is inexpensive,
packs into a tiny size and can be flipped
with a switch to be used as a webcam.

https://amzn.to/2DnRLLw

USB mics are the best solution for
recording into computers or for live
streaming. The advantage being that
digital information is being saved directly
to the computer so you can have greater
control over how the final output sounds.
You are very unlikely to get interference
or other nuisances on audio tracks. I use
the *Rode NT-USB*, it's great value and it
sounds fantastic.

https://amzn.to/3aqT4Wt

Tablets and iPads are great for writing on screen type videos. Also, many
computers come with pen and touch input. These pens are now very good
quality and give good accurate writing experiences. My experience is that the
apple pencil for the last two generations of *iPad* is the best overall experience for
accuracy and ease of writing. All of these require you to keep them charged,
with some offering wireless charging where they are stored, but because of this
they give very accurate results. Styluses for tablet screens which do not have
battery charge give a poor and inaccurate writing experience so should be
avoided, (except for quality drawing tablets which tend to have battery free
styluses and are very accurate as they are intended for use by visual artists.)

An advantage of using an *iPad* or tablet is that the entire process can happen on
one device. All the recording, narration, editing and exporting can be done
without having to transfer any files, this can significantly speed up your
workflow! However, if you are going
to edit and combine these screen
recorded clips on your computer,
this becomes a disadvantage as you
have the added step of moving the
files from your *iPad* or tablet to the
PC.

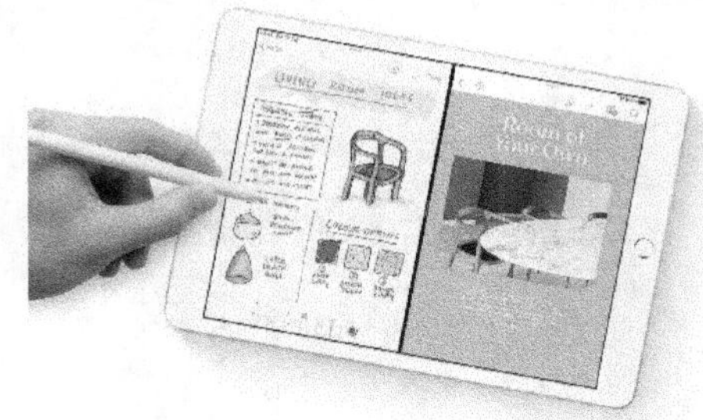

https://amzn.to/33ZDhg1

Drawing tablets make a great
addition to any computer enabling
you to write on screen when doing
the screen capture type of video. If
you are happy to use the type where
you look at a separate monitor,
then even a very large one is now
inexpensive.

https://amzn.to/3lihyGj

I'd suggest that you make sure that you get one which has a pen which doesn't
need to be recharged, because it can ruin your enthusiasm to settle down to use
something and discover that it needs to be charged! (For these, art-orientated
drawing tablets and pen displays the stylus not having a battery does not inhibit
the accuracy of the writing.) More expensive pen displays offer the best writing
experience but are large, expensive and need external power. Consider getting
one of these if you have a desktop PC set up and space on your desk for it.

Wacom are the best-known brand
and make very high-quality
products, but *Huion* and *XP Pen*
are fast catching up in terms of
quality and are certainly cheaper
options.

https://amzn.to/2DVOYK5

2i. Technical stuff (shooting)

Light, camera and sound.

The three things that matter when capturing video of any sort are: *light*, *camera* and *sound*.

To reiterate that means; plenty of light, falling on your face or whatever you are filming, a well composed locked off camera shot, and clear, loud, audible sound.

Ok, I suppose if you are screen capturing from a computer or table then light and camera aren't exactly the things you need to worry about. In these cases you could see *light* as being what the colour scheme is, and how easy to read it is or how pleasing it is to look at, and *camera* could be what you choose to show or not show to make things look pleasing and professional.

Below I'm going to give you a little more detail on how to achieve professional looking video.

Light

Flattering light can make a massive difference. Not only to how professional your output looks but also to how you will feel about yourself when you see yourself on video. This will make you feel more confident on camera the next time.

The main things to avoid are:

Too little light entirely. You get muddy, noisy looking footage from your cameras with horrible colours.

Back lit situations. This by far the most common problem and results in a face in shadow and a bright background. Always have the light falling on the face of the subject and never film with your back to a bright window.

Harsh shadows. This will make your face look really severe, it will emphasise, and elongate facial features (and you are sure to give yourself anxiety about the size of your nose!) These are generally caused by either using an overly bright, direct light source, such as a bare bulb or bright cloudless skies. Look for diffuse sources of light, such as soft boxes, windows with drawn blinds, cloudy skies (or go into the shade), or even just by reflecting your lamps off the walls or ceilings.

I've given you the gear and instructions on how to set-up studio lights in the preceding chapters. Remember the principle is; *plenty of diffuse light.*

My pro-tip here is just to spend a few minutes before you finally press record, just to have a look at the lighting of a short test clip and just think what you can change. You can do a lot by moving a little in the room, or moving a lamp a little closer or further away, and don't underestimate how useful a window is!

Camera

If your camera has manual settings in video, then you should certainly get to know them and use them. The three settings that matter are; the *iso*, the *shutter speed* and the *aperture*. Each one can make the image made on the screen brighter or darker. But they change other things too. There's loads to learn about these three settings, which are called in photography, *the exposure triangle.* But with video you should always match the shutter speed to the frame rate. Start by setting that and don't change it!

Your shutter speed should be twice the value of whatever the frame rate is. Most likely your camera will default to either 25 frames per second (fps) or 30 fps, in which case your shutter speed should be 50 (1/50th of a second) or 60 (1/60th of a second) respectively. Using this rule gives a natural motion blur and avoids jerky motion. If your camera lets you shoot at 50fps or 60fps then you should go for 100 or 120 as your shutter speeds.

Your iso should be as low as possible. This will allow the cleanest images. Higher iso numbers give more sensitivity to light, but they give you more noise and less sharp images. (And it is digital noise, which never looks good.) You should, if you have lit your scene right, be able to use iso 100 or 200 for all of your shooting!

Your aperture setting gives you the most creative control in video, so aim to use the other two settings to allow you to choose the aperture to give you the look you want. The lower the number, the wider the aperture. Wider apertures give brighter images, but shallower depth of field, so less is in focus. This can give a very pleasing separation of subject from the background. For example, an aperture of F1.8 will give you a pleasing background blur, but you may find that objects that you are referring to are out of focus. Especially if you have more than one person in a shot, you may well need to reduce the size of the aperture, increasing the depth of the field of focus and keeping both subjects in sharp focus. In this case you should look to increase your iso sensitivity of the camera sensor.

Many cameras now have the option to shoot in higher resolution modes than standard HD. This can be useful for creative edits and can future proof your work for when 4K resolution screens are the norm. But remember that the content you produce will tend to be consumed at 1080p HD resolution, (or lower), and so shooting in 4K is not totally necessary. Only shoot in one of the higher resolution modes if you feel that your computer can handle editing the footage. There is no point in having the extra pixels if it just causes editing to be a slow painful process and for you to not enjoy it or be able to do it quickly. It is true though that 4K resolution video does look great, so if your camera and computer are up to it, go for it!

The same goes for high frame rates, 50 or 60fps footage can look really smooth. It's overkill for most educational videos, but if you want to produce the highest quality, why not go for it?! Many cameras and phones will also let you record very high frame rate slow motion, and this could be really very useful for some educational niches, for example sports or dance!

Not having steady camera shots are the second easiest way to ruin a video, (after poor sound quality). I would expect that the vast majority of your shots in educational content would have the camera locked off on a tripod. But if and when you do decide to hand hold the camera, perhaps walking and talking, or filming out and about, or panning across some demo you are trying to show, you need to have a way to steady that camera.

It is impossible to watch jittery, jerky footage for more than a few moments. It looks incredibly unprofessional. Make slow purposeful movements with the camera, thinking before hand about the composition of the shot at the start and the end, and then aiming to move the camera in a smooth line between them.

My pro-tip here is to find some way to steady the shot. Brace the camera against something, or against a part of your body to stop it jittering just with your natural hand shake. Have the camera on a tripod, even when the legs aren't on the ground, the extra weight underneath the camera will act to lower the camera's centre of gravity and make it less shaky. If none of these options are available then consider a gimbal, professional steady cam, or use digital or other types of in camera or lens stabilisation.

Position your camera lens at eye level with the subject. The position of webcams on laptops has led to so many unflattering videos which are more nostrils than eyes! You will thank yourself for taking a second to get the camera to the right height when you look back and aren't worried about the double chin that seems to appear every time you open your mouth!

Framing your shot is not a rocket science, but you do need to give it some thought. There are lots of technical definitions of shots, but the two that you'll probably get most use out of are mid shots and medium close ups. A mid shot is your standard presenter shot, from the navel up, not cutting off the head. A medium close shot is essentially head and shoulders full in the frame. You can use these just to change angle and hide cuts or to emphasise certain points that you are making.

Take the time to compose your shots, the rule of thirds is a useful compositional tool, essentially split your frame into three sections horizontally and vertically and place your subject on these lines, or at points where the lines cross, or in the boxes that are created by the lines. You can see from the screenshots here, sometimes I place myself on one of the vertical lines, leaving space for text or images. This is a relaxed composition and lends itself towards explanation. Other times I place my face centrally in the frame and this gives intimacy and impact to what I am saying. This lends itself more to key points or messages in the videos.

But of course, every rule was meant to be broken! Review your footage and your uploads regularly, try new things and learn how to improve.

Sound

As a presenter you should try and keep an even tone and pace. Many clips from amateur presenters start off very loud, confident and enthusiastic but end quiet, mumbling and apologetic. Just be aware of your tone and try and keep it even. I find that not thinking too far ahead and delivering what I want to say in short sections, helps me maintain an enthusiastic, even cadence.

Not too loud, not too quiet. You should record your sound such that you are not going to lose any sounds due to clipping. This is where the sound that you are trying to record is too loud for the microphone to actually record any detail. You do this using the audio meters. You also need to avoid the audio being too quiet because if you have to raise the loudness too much in the editing software you will also be amplifying any background noise that you may have recorded in your track.

Most cameras or microphones will let you set the gain levels. Preferably set it somewhere in the -10dB range when recording. This is often shown in colour on audio meters, you want to avoid your sound being regularly in the orange or red section. If your meter doesn't have colour, then you want to see the audio meter hovering about halfway up the range as your presenter speaks. You will then bring your sound up to the correct level in your editing software later. The principle is; record quieter, because you can recover quiet audio, but you cannot recover sound that was not recorded because it was too loud.

If possible, use headphones to monitor audio so you can be sure that they aren't clipping. Monitoring using headphones will also help identify if there are any other sound sources in the room which can easily be reduced. For example; a fan in the room which can be turned off, or if you are outside and wind noise or road noise is causing the sound to be inaudible and you can just change your location to somewhere sheltered from the wind or away from the road.

Above all, make sure that you are checking your sound whilst shooting. This is the biggest annoyance in making videos, when you complete a shoot and import your footage into the editing software, and you find that your sound has made the video unusable. A whole day filming could be ruined by something as simple as the mic not being plugged in fully!

Shoot with intention.

Think about what the final product is going to look like. Imagine what you want the final video to be like and plan carefully all the things you are going to need and need to do to make it so. Plan every shot that you are going to get.

Get the gear ready the day before. Make sure cameras are charged and that all of your gear is serviceable. Tidy the studio space the day before so that you can walk straight in and get into the creative mode of work which is best for making videos. Set aside time so that you can take your time and you aren't nervously rushing to get your final shots.

Frame your shots carefully and intentionally. This is where having a second person available can be invaluable, flip screens are great, but it's harder to do all the technical stuff yourself and focus on your delivery. Look straight down the lens, not at yourself in the screen and give it your best shot.

Have fun!

Filming with a friend can also make it less intimidating and more fun. It's far easier to have a laugh and be relaxed on camera when someone else is around to laugh when you mispronounce *organism* … *again!*

A friend can help you out by being a camera operator, or by helping you know whether your explanation was good enough. And they can also keep you sane.

It's also far easier to not get worked up when things aren't going right with someone else there. A smiling, encouraging face behind the camera will help you keep a smiling confident face in front of the camera. It's also easier to get into the mode of *performing* when there is someone there to actually impress!

If you have a team for your YouTube channel you can separate the tasks in making videos so that you can be more efficient. Have one person whose job it is to make sure you are capturing all the shots you need. One person who is just thinking about the script and making sure you say everything that you need, making edits or improving content as you go. Have one person working the cameras, one person for the sound. All this leaving one person to actually perform on camera.

It takes a while to get set up to shoot so consider using batch shooting, where you have planned the content of several videos and you can film those videos all in one go. Try and compartmentalize your time in that way. One day might be the day that you shoot, and another day might be the day that you edit a batch of videos.

Keep the camera rolling, you don't need to get it all in one take. It's far easier to cut out the bits that you muddled your lines later than it is to stop and start the camera.

Above all, be reflective, and learn and improve every time. Work towards putting out content that you can be proud of. Do that and you can be confident people will watch, and your videos will perform on YouTube.

2j. Technical stuff (computer software and hardware)

Computer specifications.

Computing is another ingredient that you are going to need to get right. Whilst any laptop made in the last decade will be capable of editing a HD video, the experience will be better the higher the specs of the PC. If you are going to use an older computer, just make sure that you don't shoot video in the higher resolution, 4K mode. And, use simple, light video editing software, like *iMovie* on *Mac* or the video editor in the *photos* app on *Windows*. You'll be fine as long as you expect to do simple video edits that don't involve a lot of cuts, complex motion graphics and titles or lots of picture in picture cut screens.

In fact, most phones and tablets will do a perfectly fine job of editing videos.

However, if you want to get serious about making your videos look and sound as good as possible, it's definitely worth investing in your computer. I recommend going for a desktop PC set up for lots of reasons. If it suits you better to have one higher spec laptop, then just invest in a second monitor, a USB keyboard and mouse and a laptop stand and you can have a similar experience to a desktop computer.

To smoothly run the professional standard video editors and make complex edits you need; a multicore processor, with a high base clock speed, an SSD hard drive with a fast read and write speed, plenty of RAM and a dedicated graphics card; in that order of priority.

I'd recommending looking at these specs as a guide for a minimum video editing PC. *Intel i7 processor, 500ME SSD, 16GB RAM, Nvidia GTX 1050 Graphics.* You'd be surprised at how inexpensive that setup might be as a desktop, although you'll pay almost twice as much in a laptop form factor. There are other brands, the latest *Ryzen AMD* processors are very good, and of course *apple* make their own brand of graphics cards and processors.

Remember to look for the latest versions of processors and RAM. We are on the 10th generation of *Intel Core i* processors in 2020, so look for model names starting with a 10! The highest speed RAM currently available is the DDR4 RAM, so make sure you are getting that if you are buying new. Look for the latest *m.2 SSD* hard drives for the best performance. But again, if you have room for a desktop go for that, because it's much easier to upgrade components and the same basic computer will stay with you for a lot longer than a laptop will!

Editing software relies mainly on the processor of the computer, (CPU), so this needs to be your first priority. Secondly the editing software needs to be able to access the source video files to give you smooth playback whilst editing, so hard drive read and write speed is your second priority. Plenty of fast RAM is a next priority as this is where the computer stores the working programme files for all the apps that you have open. Lastly a high spec graphics card, (GPU) will speed up playback, any hardware accelerated or 3D graphics you add, and will speed up video exporting times, typically with GPUs look for more cores and VRAM.

The other key thing to get right is screen real estate. You should look to get two monitors for your desktop computer to give you room to have multiple windows open at one time. This will speed up your editing giving you a view of your video timeline, the output (preview) monitor and all of the other editing controls at the same time.

You'll also want to invest in some good quality speakers or a good pair of over ear headphones. This is not just about sound quality for playback but is more about being able to hear the full audible range of your video clips when editing. Built in speakers on monitors or laptops tend to lack the base frequencies. Without these you may not hear whilst editing distracting noise or sounds which could be present in your soundtrack and so very distracting to the viewer.

Editing software.

On Windows there is a basic video editor in the *photos* app, you can also still get *Windows Movie Maker* for free in the apps store. On Mac OS you can have *iMovie* for free. Both are absolutely fine for basic editing, and if you've never edited a video before start there. Many education YouTube channels have used these simple editing suites for the majority of their videos.

By keeping things simple, you'll be able to learn the processes of trimming and constructing a timeline without many features to get in the way! Follow my tutorial in the chapter "basic video editing" to learn an efficient workflow.

If you are reading this book though you are probably interested in making your videos with higher production value. In which case, you'll quickly outgrow the simple options and using a professional video editor is going to be absolutely necessary.

There are three main options for you, *da Vinci Resolve*, *Final Cut* and *Adobe Premiere Pro*. There is a steep learning curve for all professional video editing suites, but luckily there are lots of educational YouTube channels dedicated to teaching you how to use them!

Da Vinci Resolve is a fully featured professional editing suite for absolutely nothing. There is a professional paid version, but this is not necessary unless you are going to work in a large team and need to put out cinema quality videos. This is a great option for anyone looking to get started with more advanced editing techniques but who doesn't wish to commit to paying for a particular programme. *Da Vinci Resolve* works on both PC and Mac.

Final Cut Pro is *apple's* professional video editing software and so is only available on Mac. I haven't personally used this editing software as I don't use Mac computers. However, it is a great option if you use Mac computers. In general *apple* software can be relied upon to work great on *apple* computers!

Adobe Premiere Pro comes as part of the *Adobe Creative Cloud (CC)* suite of apps. These can be bought by subscription, and although this is not cheap, you can get a large discount if you can prove that you are an educator! It's what I use for many reasons but mainly because I can rely on it to have a way to do any creative edit that I could think of. There is a steep learning curve but there are thousands of tutorials to get you started using the software and you'll be up and running in no time. You'll become confident after completing a few videos with it.

One of the main benefits of going with a subscription to *Adobe CC* are the other parts of the *CC* suite desktop and mobile apps. As well as this you get cloud storage of assets that you use regularly which you can access in any of their applications. You can save and sync projects to the cloud and access and edit them on multiple devices!

For example, I often shoot quick videos on my phone, put them into *Adobe Premiere Rush* app on my phone. I start to cut, sequence and add titles on my phone whenever I get a few minutes during my day, before tidying up the sound, adding background music and a few extra cut screens and exporting the finished video on my desktop PC at a later date.

I recommend *Adobe CC* if you want to get serious about the whole of your online education brand, as well as if you are creative and want to edit photos in *Lightroom* or *Photoshop*. *Adobe CC* has apps to make websites, apps to layout books, apps to paint, apps to make music, even apps to make apps! I use the *Adobe Spark Post* app on my phone to make all my thumbnails and they look great in seconds. The last powerful app I'll mention is *Adobe After Effects* which is their massively powerful 3D special effects editor. If you are looking to make your videos look really serious, this is the app for you.

Other Software.

MS PowerPoint (and the rest of the *MS Office* suite) are being updated all the time and are becoming more and more useful for video content creators. *PowerPoint* has a built in video creation function which lets you record narrations, slide timings and animations, webcam video footage and *Microsoft Ink* (digital pen annotations), and to export the file as a video which you can either upload directly or use as part of your final video edit.

You can probably get a full copy of *MS Office Professional* from your workplace for free to install on your home computers. If not, then *Office 365 Home* has all the features that you will need and is a pretty affordable subscription service now. It often comes packaged with other products like web hosting or with new computers, so look out for that as a great value way to get office. Aside from that *Word* and *Excel* are absolutely industry standard and I wouldn't want to be without either of them.

OBS is designed to put out live streamed content but you can also record your screen, a window, a webpage, your webcam, overlay text, even pre-load transitions. Essentially it is a digital, live television mixing studio, you could use it for very powerful results. It is not an intuitive user interface at first but once you get used to it it is a very easy piece of software to use. Once again there are lots of tutorials out there on YouTube to show you how to get set up with it.

Zoom and *MS Teams* will also let you share presentations, and record content sharing your screen and your webcam at the same time and by switching between them, but they give you fewer creative options than *OBS*.

Screen recorders are now built into *iOS* devices and *Android* devices. Windows comes with a built-in screen recorder which you can access at any time by pressing the "windows + g" keys.

MS Whiteboard and *apple notes* or *notability* on the *iPad* are both very good ways to write on the screen and record using screen capture software. The best all round software for making videos on *iPad* is probably *Explain Everything*. This gives you an infinite whiteboard and lots of other creative tools for making neat looking explainer videos.

On your phone, *iPad* or *Android* tablet there are a range of mobile editors to choose from. *iMovie* is fine and there is a free version for you to use. If you are on *Android* perhaps try *Kinemaster* which I find has the best feature set and is actually pretty fun to use. *Adobe Premiere Rush* is in my opinion the best mobile editor, although it is not without its bugs, this is certainly the best if you are using the other *Adobe* products to make your channel.

2k. Basic video editing

Cut out the ums and errs.

YouTube audiences aren't used to videos where people *um*… and *err*…. They aren't going to hang around while you write and they aren't going to trust someone who rambles on.

There's loads to learn in editing, it can be time-consuming, but it's where you make your video into something valuable. Whilst it's true that many teachers can turn on the visualiser and chat through their topic it is the choices you make in the editing process will mean the difference between a quality product or not.

Before reading this chapter, make sure that you have completed the activity in the Chapter 1c "Making your first video."

Workflow.

In all my edits I follow this simple order of processes. Whichever software you chose to use, you can still follow this basic sequence of tasks. Following this sequence will save you time as one process can impact another. For example, if you cut before you colour, you have to colour for every clip!

1. Assembly
2. Audio
3. Colour
4. Cutting
5. Graphics
6. Sounds
7. Export

These are generic instructions which should work with any video editing software. Software all have different sets of features, so some features may be missing from the software you choose to use. Or the feature may have different names. Google questions like *how do I* … and you will no doubt find specific answers to show how you can achieve the same thing in your software of choice. Also, guess what, YouTube is full of tutorials explaining how to get things done in any video editing software!

1. Assembly

This simply means putting your clips you have recorded into a timeline. Make sure you have all the shots and all the audio into the editing software in the rough order that you want them to appear. You can do a little rough cutting here, if you know that there's a big chunk that you don't want to use, or where you messed up your lines.

Try to be organised when you plan and shoot your videos so that this step takes as little time as possible. As you learn you'll get better at doing this and organising your footage so that you aren't having to look around your hard drive later on in the process for that one clip that you thought you'd use to illustrate your point. The better planned that you are before you shoot so your footage the easier this assembly step will be. You can write a shot list when you are planning as this will help you avoid getting to the edit and thinking *I wish I'd filmed that!*

2. Audio

Make sure your voice is loud enough, you want the highest peaks in your audio tracks to be around -3db. (Note lower volumes are given negative values in dB, with -50 being basically not audible at all.)

Many editing softwares have automatic settings or voice enhancement settings. Look for an auto volume or the tool to set audio gain, for example "set audio peaks to -3db" is a good way to quickly make sure that everything is loud enough for your audience. Use these and listen to your tracks to check that you are happy with the results. If there are sections where your voice is louder or quieter there are ways to adjust the volume for individual sections if your clips. Look for an audio levels tool which allows you to make these adjustments.

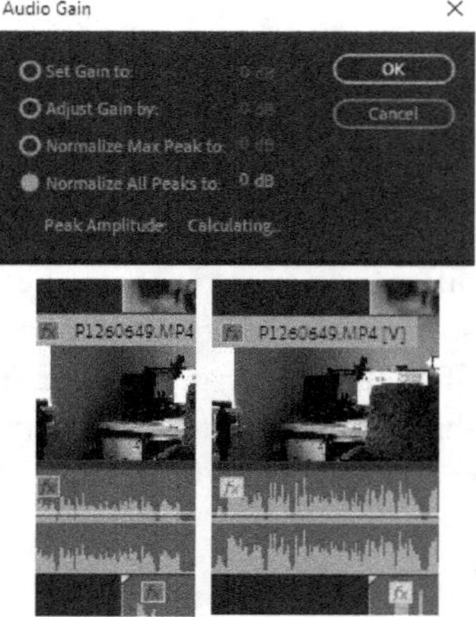

During this stage, if your editing software has the function, apply compression. This is the trick that broadcasters use to make presenters' voices sound buttery smooth and pleasant to listen to. Compression brings up the volume of the quiet sound and reduces the volume of the higher sounds. This means that you get rid of the sudden changes in volume that we all naturally do when we speak. The effect is that voices sound less jarring, as you don't get sudden increases in volume. If you have the choice apply "broadcast compression" and many softwares have different options for male or female voices which boost the base frequencies different amounts.

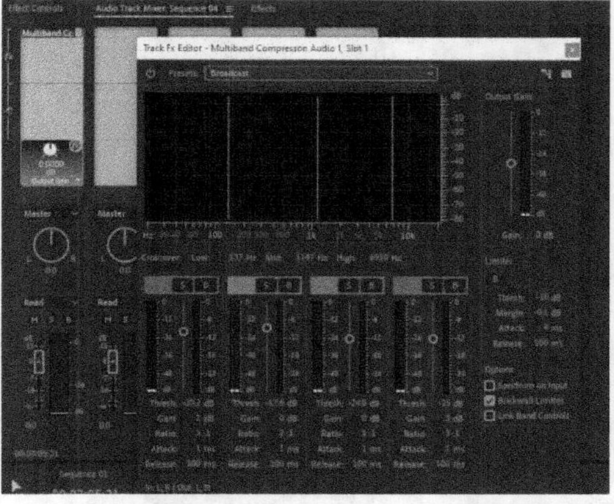

Apply noise reduction if you need it. Most editing softwares have the option for background noise reduction. Some are very smart and analyse the audio track to just reduce the sounds which are not the speaker's voice but you may still need to adjust the settings to get something which sounds natural. Listen to the clip back once you've applied the effect though because often audio with noise reduction applied can sometimes sound a little overly digitised and it might be better just to put up with the noise!

Mute or lower the volume of clips where you aren't taking. You don't want the background sound from clips where you are just showing a demonstration or during clips of you writing or drawing. You can cover these silences with background music later if you like.

You aren't putting background music or sound effects in at this point. That comes later. The aim of this section is just to make sure that everything that should be audible is loud and clear and everything which shouldn't be is muted.

3. Colours

This can be as simple as applying filters, or as involved as a full-on colour grade using scopes and histograms to maximise the dynamic range of your camera.

Don't overdo it to the point where it becomes distracting. But do a little until you are pleased with the "look" of your footage. Use a consistent look which suits your channel or the content of the video. Planning colour schemes in advance can help give a consistent feel. Perhaps, for example, you like to use a pastel set of highlighters in your videos, you could also wear pastel shades of clothes in the videos, and mute any saturated colours in the edit. Or if you are making a video about van Gogh's changing pallet when he lived to Paris perhaps your filters can become brighter and warmer, and maybe you wear complimentary colours for this video! This can be reflected in the colour filters you apply to your footage.

I know that this is not massively important to an education channel, after all no one ever learned anything because of the colour scheme, but avoid using footage which is just as the camera saw it. Every TV show or movie you've ever seen has had filters applied to the footage. Skipping this step is an easy way to make you video look "unprofessional".

4. Cutting

Now's the time to complete the final cut. The aim is to produce a slick viewer experience where there are no large silent periods of time and you've cut out any superfluous chat! I spend quite a bit of time doing this for all my videos and I think it's worth it.

You need to sound like an authority on what you are presenting to be trusted. If you make a mistake, cut it out! I cut out all my *ums…* and *errs…*, and any large pauses. It's reasonably quick to do because you can often see quiet bits, or buts where you've stopped and started on your audio waveform on the timeline.

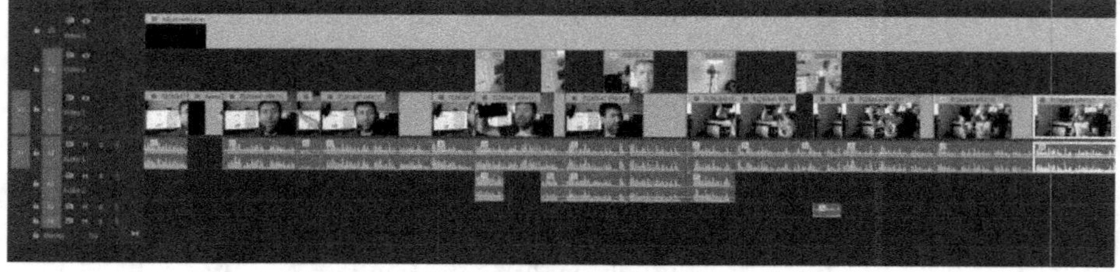

Getting used to cutting out mistakes and pauses can be really useful to you as a presenter as you can just leave the camera rolling whilst you think about what you are going to say next, safe in the knowledge that you are going to just chop that pause out later.

You can cover cuts in video by using B-roll or free stock footage, or even reframing the shot if you're shooting in 4K. Then no-one will ever know you messed up, and you look and sound super smart! Don't worry if you have nothing to cover the cut though, as using "jump cuts" (i.e. cutting straight from one moment to the next) is very normal on YouTube and doesn't look or sound so bad that people will stop watching.

Make sure you are happy with the sequence at this point and really be ruthless about getting rid of unnecessary talk. The aim is to end up with a timeline which is engaging and gives the viewer no time in which to get bored and look for the next video! Unfortunately, this the cause of, and solution to, the short attention spans of viewers online!

5. Graphics

This is where you add the text and images that you need to to make your point come across strongly. I say; *this is where your PowerPoint skills come in.* What I mean by that is as a teacher or educator you know what you need to show to kids. When you are editing you need to select the visual elements that need

to be included in order for your audience to understand what is being explained to them. You know what key words or key phrases you need to put in screen whilst you talk to enable them to get the language skills to succeed in each topic. You know which diagrams they need to be familiar with. And you know which photographs are great for engaging them in a particular topic!

You can display these as text over the screen as you talk, or in separate slides with your voice over the top. It's a good idea to frame yourself to one side of the screen so that you can use the other side of the screen for text and images without covering your face.

As with all editing, the better you plan your ideas before you press record the easier it all comes together in the edit. Another idea is to cover the entire screen with a text or image to disguise those "jump cuts"!

6. Sounds

I like to use background music in my videos. Get it right and it can be one of the most powerful ways to convey a mood, a feeling and keep people engaged. Get it wrong and it could be very distracting and make your voice impossible to follow. (I have done both in the past!)

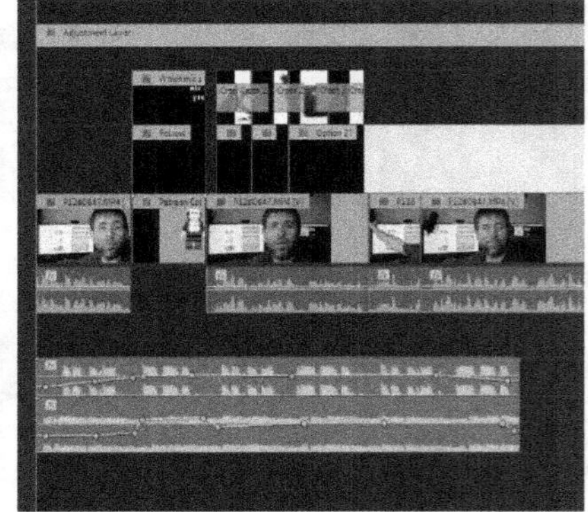

If you are not sure then perhaps try just a short jingle over the intro and outros of your video and leave the speaking parts just with your voice. You could also try very short phrases of music as a way to transition from one subtopic to another. This, coupled with a title, is a good way to signify that you're done with one thing and are going to start to talk about something new.

Choose simple melodic tracks, with no lyrics. Even better pick tracks which don't have drums and avoid instruments similar in pitch to your voice, so they aren't competing with you for attention.

Again, you cannot just use any music for copyright reasons so make sure that music you choose is used fairly under licence or you know is free to use on YouTube. YouTube provides a library of copyright and royalty free music and sound effects which you can find in the YouTube studio, the part of the website where you do all your uploads and find your analytics.

Place your music track below your speaking parts and reduce the volume down to around -20db. As a rule, do not go above -14db as it will start to be difficult to hear your voice. You can increase the volume of the music over parts of the video where you are not speaking and lower the volume when you are. This is called "ducking". Many video editing softwares can do this automatically.

Sound design is one of the most powerful aspects of a good edit and something which can make you work feel more professional. Sound effects other than music can also give an additional impact and emphasis to what you are saying. Remember to use them sparingly and well timed so that they don't become distracting.

7. Export

Before uploading and sharing your video you need to export it as a video file. Whilst it is in the video editor it is only viewable by that video editing software. It is building a preview that you can watch back by referencing all the individual files and showing what the exported video will look like.

There are often many different options to choose when exporting, and you cannot go far wrong, but you just need to make sure a couple of things are checked.

If there is a YouTube 1080p video pre-set, then you can just use that and be confident it will upload to YouTube with no issues.

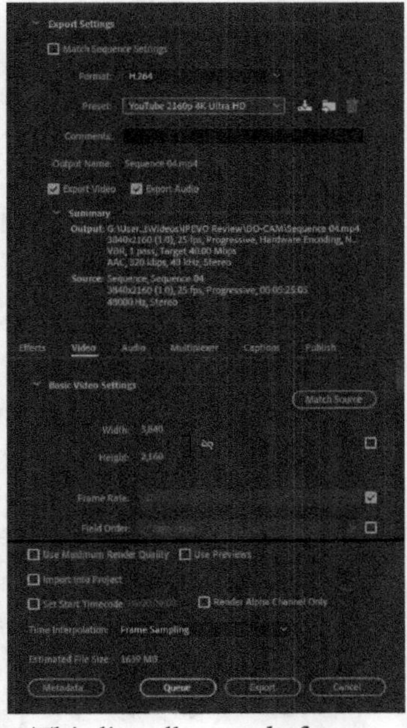

Export in the best possible quality, but not higher than whatever the quality of footage you used. YouTube will create its own lower quality files to make streaming seamless for slower connections. So, if you filmed in 4K go ahead and export in 4K, if you filmed in 1080p (full HD) then go ahead and export in 1080p. If you have no idea, then export in 1080p, that's the most common screen resolution in 2020!

You may have the option to choose the video file format. *.mp4* is the most common video file type. This is fine, *.avi*, *.mov*, and *.wmv* are also commonly recognised file formats.

You may have the option to choose a video codec. This literally stands for code-decode. A codec is like a cypher which the computer uses to translate the file from ones and zeros into pixel brightness and colour. The codec allows the video file to be smaller than it would be if it were a series of full photos, 25 every second. *H.264* is the most common video codec, so if you have the option of that go with it. You won't really need to export in anything else for YouTube, as many others are designed for higher quality playback formats, and YouTube is going to compress your video in any case.

Lastly if you can choose a frame rate, try and match the same frame rate (frames per second, of FPS) that you filmed in. If you used your smartphone it is likely to be 30fps, if you used a digital camera in the UK it will likely be 25fps, (in the US 30fps. The difference is linked to our power lines and traditional TV broadcast frequencies.)

You can find this information by looking at the "properties" of the video files that you recorded and the timeline or sequence that you've been working in.

Chose the highest sound quality, but again no higher than you recorded at. Again you can find details by right clicking the file and selecting "properties", (or "get info" on Mac.)

Now hit export. It's likely to take a few minutes, even on a powerful machine, so go grab a drink and read the upload chapter!

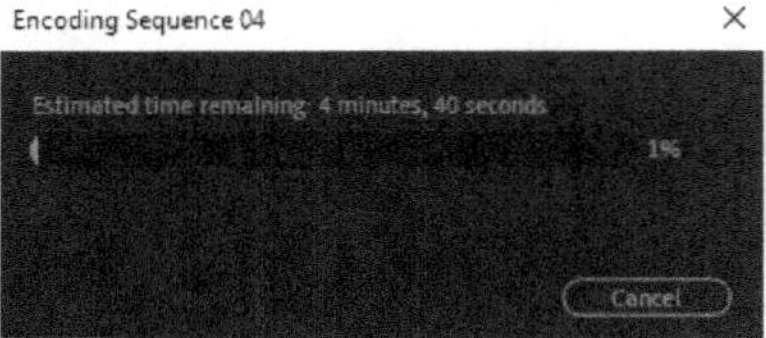

Activity: Follow this editing workflow as described in this chapter for your next three videos.

Set aside plenty of time to do your first edits. Expect those edits to take a little longer than they will take once you have learned your way around the software. Use the extra time that you've allocated to editing to research tools and tips for editing with your editing software. I vastly recommend that you learn to use the keyboard shortcuts for editing as this will save you loads of time.

Try to use the same workflow next time you edit a video but try to speed up a little now that you are learning your way around the editing software. Between each edit watch your video several times and reflect on what you do and do not like. Also think about how to streamline the process of editing videos for yourself and your videos.

Decide on what is important to you in the edit and what is not. Try and edit your next videos as quickly as possible whilst still getting to a standard that you are happy with. Aim for it to take less than an hour to edit a five minute video.

---

21. Blended learning

My experience of blended learning.

In the last five years I have used blended learning in my classroom. I've had massive success and I've had failures. In this chapter I'll tell you everything I've learned.

The biggest lesson that I've learned about it is that blended learning requires keen engagement from both the teacher and from the class. One way to show that engagement from your end, the teacher's end, is to make your own YouTube video resources rather than simply to set existing videos. This gives authenticity and the feeling of a programme tailored by you, for the students in your classes. Aside from this, students love to hear their own teacher's voice.

You are showing willing to engage with your class at a time they choose, rather than forcing them to listen to you for an hour at the time when the timetable says they should be ready to listen. And you allow yourself and your teaching style to be adaptive and responsive to the needs of your learners. For example if they struggle with a concept and need your expert guidance though it, you've freed up classroom time by delivering some material at home.

In my experience there are three key things that you need to get right to make a success of blended learning. You have to:

- Teach them how to learn from videos.
- Make a decision between the flipped and traditional models of teaching and learning for every objective and for every group.
- Assess what they've learned out of the classroom with great precision at the start of lessons to ensure misconceptions aren't perpetuated.

A blend of two models.

I find this diagram a useful way to imagine the process of selecting which model you are choosing for each objective and for each

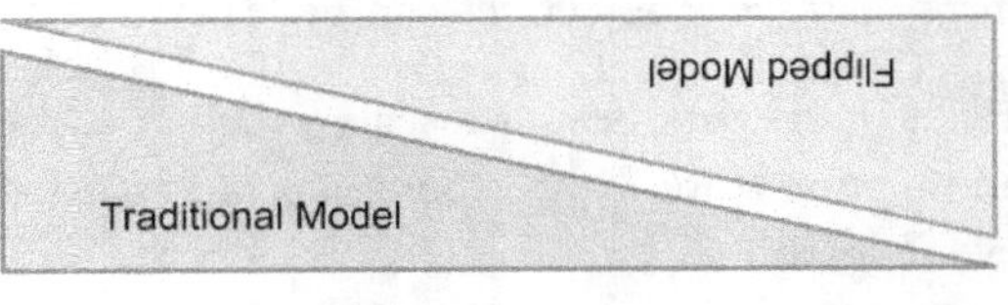

group. It's a sliding scale of the blend between the flipped and the traditional model of teaching and learning. It's not an all or nothing choice, between explanation delivered at home and explanation disseminated in a classroom.

There are reasons to teach using a flipped class model and reasons to teach in a traditional manner.

You can, for some objectives, for some groups, expect them to learn entirely on their own at home. You can check this at the start of the lesson, then move straight into the higher order skills in the topic you are covering.

For this same objective, but for a different class you may decide you to entirely teach from the front of your classroom, carefully using their feedback to ensure you are carrying all of them through your explanation entirely. For a third group you may decide that they should see the flipped resources, but also know that you'll need to go over the ideas at the start of the lesson.

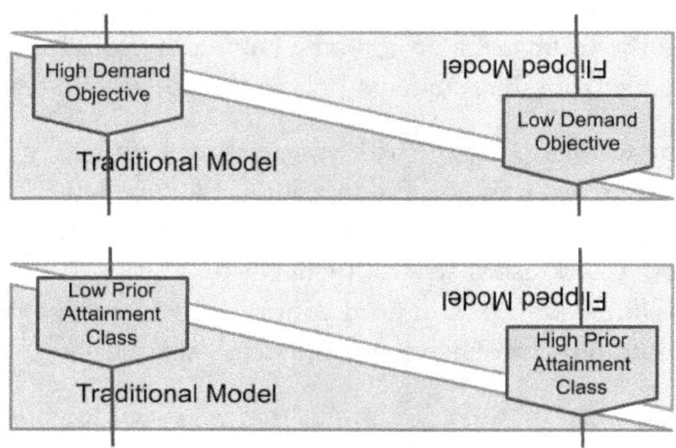

You can imagine each objective and each class as a slider on the scale between the flipped and traditional models of learning.

Making the decision.

The theory of blended learning is tied to the taxonomic demand of learning objectives. However, it is an oversimplification to suggest that all *state, describe* or *explain* objectives are suitable to be learned at home. Or that none of the *analysis* or *evaluate* objectives can be learned at home.

It really does work best as a scale which you, the educator, are constantly manipulating using your experience and assessment of the students and what they are learning.

I would though suggest that videos are better suited to *describe* and *explain* type objectives.

A well selected, blended lesson might be structured as follows. Students learn key foundational definitions and descriptive vocabulary at home. The teacher begins the lesson with a quiz. From this they intervene and address any misconceptions which arise from the quiz. The lesson moves swiftly on to the higher order knowledge, understanding and skills, or can be reshaped to consolidate what was not learned by the foundational home learning.

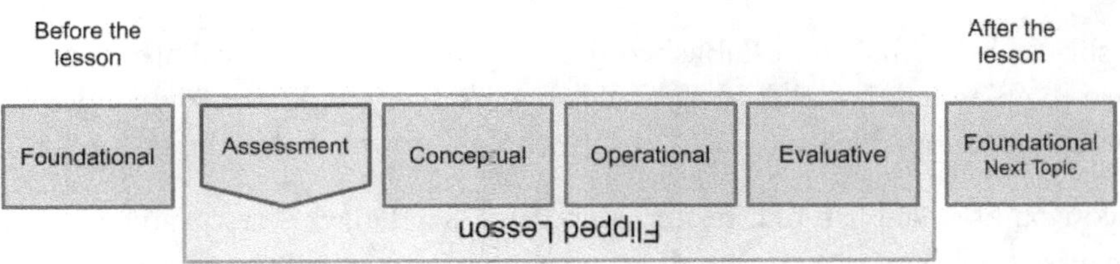

This diagram uses the simplified taxonomy of *foundational* to *evaluative* objectives.

It's important to note that the blended lesson allows for a decision to be made to revert to a traditional model. Where the assessment shows that in fact the class have not understood the content of the flipped resources, the teacher can take the time to address this.

The fundamental idea of flipped lessons is that students are doing the easiest, most accessible learning at home, where they do not have access to support. And they do the hardest, most opaque learning in school where the teachers can carefully reshape and personalise the learning. This makes time for evaluative learning within the lesson, which they may struggle to access for homework.

Where blended learning differs from flipped learning is that there is no rejection of a traditional style of teaching and learning. In blended learning there is a place for both the flipped *and* the traditional models of teaching and learning. The benefits of, for example; using homework to consolidate learning, or of the carefully sequenced and managed teacher explanation, are accommodated in the model. It is all part of the process of selection of teaching and learning model for each objective and each class.

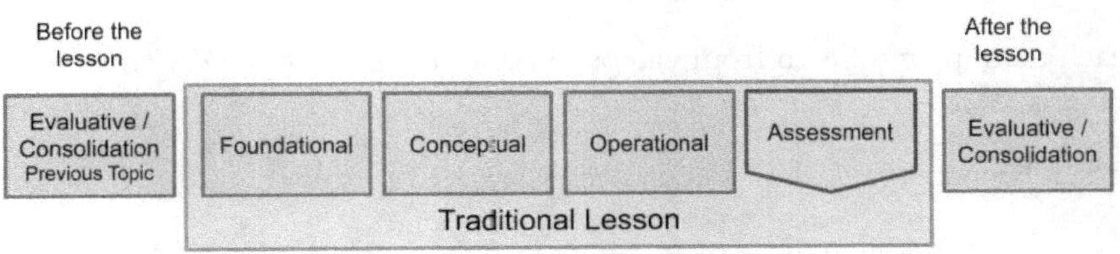

Where YouTube fits in.

Integrating your educational YouTube videos into your own classroom practice, or your own corporate learning, is where it really gets rewarding. In the years I've followed a blended learning model my most successful groups are those that I've managed to carry through the age groups. My least successful groups with blended learning are those where I've tried to impose a new style of learning on a group in a year when they are going to sit exams.

In short where I haven't established the trust in me or in the use of videos to learn the blended model fails. I would suggest that you do not try blended learning, or flipped learning, in a group who are not ready for the challenge.

If you cannot establish that relationship there is a danger that a blame culture can arise. Students may set up themselves to blame your style of teaching for their own failure in their exams.

Where I have been able to build a relationship with a group, I have been able to get them confident learning in this way. I have been able to get them to take responsibility and to be interested in physics. There was a joy in challenge, and a positive atmosphere, where kids were determined to achieve their best.

When you get it to be part of a culture of a group even those who aren't very skilled or engaged are still better equipped to take responsibility for their own home learning when it gets nearer the exams.

Remember that you must teach them *how* to learn in new this way. You must teach them the advantages of learning from videos, of taking responsibility of their own learning and demonstrate how much faster you can go when they cover foundational knowledge and understanding at home on their own. Then you must show them that you can do more exciting, more engaging, higher level activities in class.

Teach them how to study from videos.

The advantages of learning from videos seem obvious, but they aren't to all students, so make them clear!

Teach them how to learn from videos! I say to my groups, *you don't watch an educational video. You study it.*

Then it becomes clear the video is a resource, like any other.

Well-made videos are more engaging than books or webpages, and they can cover material rapidly and with carefully sequenced explanations, but they are not entertainment. Students need to remember to close other browser tabs, put away other screens and re-watch sections where they didn't follow the explanation first time.

These are all things which most people would do automatically if learning from a textbook, but it isn't the natural and normal way they use YouTube.

They need to also know not to be tempted away from the video you've chosen or made for them! YouTube is set up to be a distracting environment, that when the attention wanders from one video, it is immediately directed to the next!

If it helps them, they should be encouraged to make notes. Better than this is a short quiz accompanying the video to check that they are getting the right information. I'm always amazed that students can watch a video which repeats one piece of key learning three or four times, and they have latched on to the interesting context of the explanation as being the most important part of the video. I tend to make short, three question quizzes to accompany my videos when I share them with a class. This just ensures that they are looking out for the three key points that I want them to know well at the start of the lesson.

Assessment for learning in a blended model.

In practice the best way to employ blended learning is to think of it as a decision you make *for each objective and for each group of students* between a flipped classroom and a traditional classroom. This takes a good deal of forward planning at first but becomes a habit after a while.

Think about the objectives that you must cover in a week. Divide them into two groups. Those that you feel are simple enough for the students to cover on their own out of the classroom, and those that will need your careful construction and careful checking of student progress in the classroom.

Choose to "flip" the ones that they can get on their own and retain those that you don't think they can understand on their own to be taught in the classroom; i.e. choose where on the scale of blended learning you will place each objective. Set your flipped learning homework and remember to explain how to use the resources and how you intend to assess their learning of the flipped content at the start to the lesson they come into.

Remember this decision is not as simple as; *the lower on Bloom's taxonomy the more likely it is to be accessible at home.* Some knowledge and understanding is so abstract that you're far better to establish the knowledge and understanding in the classroom and perhaps give them the practice to take home.

Best practice with blended learning is to have some sort of entry test, between three and five simple questions perhaps at the start of the lesson or before the lesson for homework. This establishes for you whether they have grasped the foundational content that was delivered in your video at home.

With this assessment information you gauge your start point and their start point for the lesson. Perhaps you find that your class can go faster than you think. Or perhaps they have flunked the test and they need to spend the lesson getting to grips with what you thought was quite simple. Perhaps you use the assessment data to group them as to who can continue with the analysis activity and who you should be focusing on a consolidation task.

Activity: Take the objectives for your next week's teaching. Decide which ones you will carefully cover in class and decide which ones you will set for home learning.

Plan and make videos to cover the home learning and plan the in-class activities to cover the in-class learning.

Before setting them evaluate the expected effectiveness of those videos for delivering the home learning. Alter them or plan in class interventions for those who do not achieve those objectives using those materials. Perhaps there is just a few things you can say the lesson before a class watches a video to ensure they don't get misunderstandings from it. Or perhaps you have a quick set of questions at the start of a lesson to judge whether you need to go over that flipped content again.

Evaluate the impact of the learning that occurred as soon as possible afterwards.

2m. Advanced video skills and techniques

Aim for the highest quality.

Whilst all that is needed for education channels to succeed on YouTube is "good enough" video production, quality production will help to inspire confidence in your audience. Confidence is what you need if they are going to choose your video over someone else's in the future.

Making videos is fun and learning new skills is fun. Enjoy the process of learning about video production and do whatever you can to increase the quality of your content, without it taking too much time such that you don't put out videos on a regular schedule.

There are some things that you should know about video editing that will speed you up:

It's probably a pre-set. If something in another person's video looks amazing, it's probably a pre-set effect, pre-set transition, pre-set title, pre-set colour filter, or maybe a pre-set with just a few small tweaks. Look for the transitions, and effects which come built into your editing software and use these rather than making your own every time.

Speed up your edits by learning how professionals use the editing software. The mouse is rarely the fastest way to operate the computer, so learn the keyboard shortcuts for things like cut, ripple delete and trim. If you make similar changes to a whole load of clips speed yourself up by copying and pasting attributes. Also use the audio track waveform to see where speech starts and stops to speed up your cutting.

Batch plan, film and edit videos. This can make production faster, more streamlined and also improve the quality and consistency of your videos. Four videos is a manageable number, but really you could do as many as ten in one production cycle. Once you have set up your studio and camera equipment go ahead and record four videos in one session. Then edit them all in one long editing session. You can then upload them all at once and schedule them to become public on a weekly basis.

In this chapter I am going to give you a few ideas on how you can improve your video production. These aren't full tutorials that you can follow but just ideas to get you thinking. For all you'll be able to find plenty of how to videos on YouTube.

Green screen.

If you've been using *zoom* or *MS Teams* recently for meetings, or if you've ever seen a weather report, you'll know what I mean by the effect of replacing your background. You can do this with most webcams and an app like *zoom* but it won't always give you the most consistent results, and the possibility of some digital artefacts making your video look unprofessional.

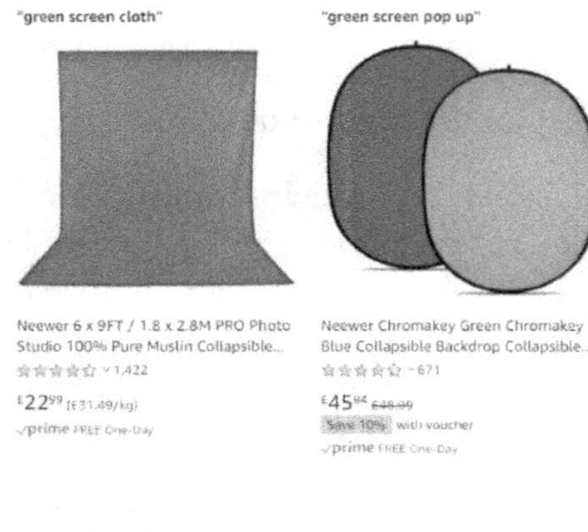

This can be improved by using an actual green screen. There are some inexpensive options. You should pick either the framed full backdrop or the pop-up type depending on whether you have a permanent studio set up or you'll need to move from place to place.

To get the best results with your green screen try and light the screen evenly so that you have one consistent colour and tone recorded across the background. And of course, try not to wear the same colour as your background!

The technical name for green screen effects is "chroma key" or "colour keying" and it works better in the more professional video editing software like *Adobe Premiere Pro*. *OBS* also has the option to remove your background, which is great as you can do it during live streams. But it is not quite as easy to use or reliable as the more fully featured editing suites.

Picture in Picture.

Picture in picture is the name given to any effect where you are showing one video at the same time as another. It's something that I use quite a lot in my videos if I want to show a demo I've recorded, make reference to another one of my videos or include some stock or public domain footage that I have found.

My pro-tip here is that you plan to do it. So that you leave space on one side of your shot so that you can fit in your picture-in picture.

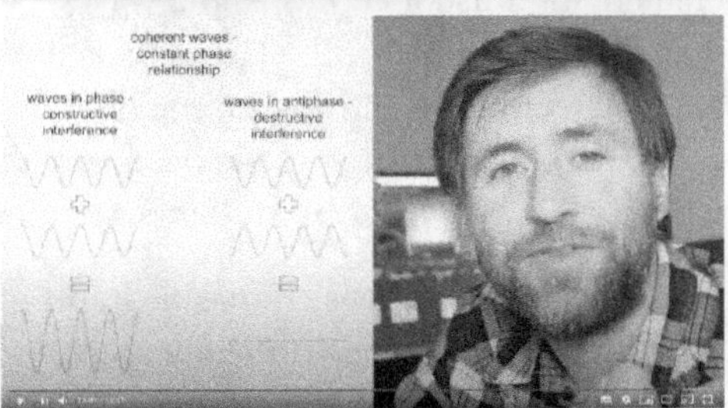

Most editing softwares, even basic ones on phones or tablets will let you do this. Some people might say that this can be distracting, but I think that it makes the video more visually appealing. It's engaging to be able to see faces as they talk and it is worth displaying demos, diagrams and animations on screen at the same time as you are talking about them.

If you use video as a picture in picture, do not forget to mute it or turn its volume down if you want people to continue to hear what you are saying in your main talking head shot.

Versa videos.

This is one of the most fun type of videos and is probably best for a video chatting through an idea rather than a detailed tutorial. It's actually incredibly simple to do, and this example I shot and edited entirely on my phone.

To do this have one locked off camera shot, using fixed manual focus is best so that the camera shot stays exactly the same. Record yourself having one side of the conversation including nodding along or reacting to what the *other person* is saying. Then record the other side of the conversation in the other position in the shot. You don't have to get timing perfect as you can speed up, slow down or cut the quiet sections to match the timing of the speaking parts. This looks fine as the viewer tends to focus on the person on a screen who is talking rather than the person reacting, so it shouldn't look odd if you are nodding slowly.

An education channel that uses this technique to really good effect is *Flipping Physics*. Jon teaches his "class" lessons, and they participate by asking questions. In this way Jon makes use of the educational technique of questioning and challenging misconceptions in a way

which is really powerful. The class is in fact himself cloned three times. This is no easy technique and the journey to complete all of the video lessons for his course in this consistent style has been a long one. But he now has a library which will be enjoyed by students for years to come.

He uses the techniques of masking and blending layers of videos to build up a seamless image where you really could believe that he has three identical brothers. As you can see he uses different clothes to give you a sense of the characters of his three *students*. As a viewer you can imagine yourself to be involved as one of *Billy, Bobby and Bo*, who reflect the characteristics of Jon's audience.

Flipping Physics is a great example of an educational channel which has grown because of the way it caters for the needs of a specific audience. They can relate to the videos and each one has massive engagement. Commit to quality and YouTube will reward you. I am pleased to say I feature as a guest in one of these excellent videos!

B Roll.

"B roll" is the term given by filmmakers to the extra shots that can be used in videos to add atmosphere, context and visual interest. For talking head videos, they add much needed variation from the simple mid shot of the presenter. They can also be used to cover cuts, where you have perhaps got a line wrong and need to cut out a section of video and wish it to appear that you were just talking continuously. They can also be used as video transitions between clips.

There are a few ways to achieve this. You could have a second camera, that could be filming items that you are discussing, or it could be a shot of the whiteboard you are writing on as you talk. It could even be a recording of a screen if you are using a presentation or writing on a screen. It could also be a second shot of you from a different angle and with a different field of view.

116

If you only have one camera however then just make a note to capture a few seconds of extra shots of what you are discussing, demos that you are showing or anything which adds context and texture to your video. B roll footage is a great way to keep a viewer engaged in your videos.

You can also use stock footage as B roll if it makes sense. *Making a history video about castles?* Here's a good clip from *pexels.com* which you can use for free with no royalty or copyright worries! Talking about coral reefs in a marine biology video? Here's some 4K footage of tropical fish on a coral reef from *pixabay.com* which you need no licence to use! You can use most materials that have creative commons licences in your videos as long as you are licencing your own videos in the same way. Every licence is different however and many require attribution so just be aware of this.

You can't just use anything on YouTube, you need to be sure that you either have permission to use something or that you are using an image or video under fair use. Mostly, as our use is for education, you will not be impinging on others copyright, unless their use was also for education!

If you have any aspirations to one day monetise your channel, I would strongly recommend you make and use your own B roll to avoid copyright issues arising later! Make a habit of taking out your phone or your camera to capture short clips of things that you might use at a later date. In this way you'll build up a sort of B roll library that you can include in your videos. You can also look back at your own videos and use short clips of those to add B roll to new videos that you are making on related topics.

Cuts and transitions.

Watch any TV or video show and notice how long any one clip, any one scene, is actually on the screen for. Unless for dramatic effect, you'll find that the shot tends change around every 2-6 seconds. You hardly notice, because the cuts are done so well. Although you do not need to go to this extreme for educational YouTube, you should be aware that this is what people are used to, and that it will almost seem unnatural if it doesn't happen.

I looked at my most recent edit and I had cut 16 times in the first minute. In the second and third minutes I cut less frequently, but none the less there is not one clip in the video which is unchanged for more than 15 seconds. Cutting at a high frequency like this, especially at the beginning of a video, can really help to keep people engaged.

On YouTube the most common cut is the "jump cut". This is where one clip ends and another begins. This is totally fine, absolutely normal on YouTube, and can be used to good effect. It is by far the easiest and quickest cut to do because you just have to cut the clip and put the next one straight after it.

Jump cuts do tend to give a sort of frenetic energy to a video though, so you may wish to consider other ways of making transitions. Have a look through the pre-sets in your editing software and see if there are any that suit your style of video. Just be aware that any kind of 3D wipe, or checkerboard, or complicated transition often gives the air of an amateur rather than a pro. Go for simple classics like a "crossfade" or "dip to black" as these are less intrusive and jarring.

It's also worth considering the transition of the soundtrack, if your sound jumps from loud to quiet every time you cut from one clip to the next, this can be jarring. Try to use a similar volume for all of your clips, and if you cannot match them well, then use a cross fade, or a J or an L cut.

J cuts and L cuts are ways of overlapping the audio with another clip. It's an idea from filmmaking where you want to linger on someone's face as another person starts talking. They get their names from the shapes that are created in the timeline by the cut. If the audio for the next clip overlaps the preceding clip this is a J cut. If the audio from the preceding clip overlaps the next clip, this is an L cut. This is all about smoothly leading the viewer into the next scene, subtly emphasising either the coming scene or the previous one. These can be used to build excitement and suspense in the movies, but for us in education, they are more about keeping viewers engaged.

As an advanced editor you should see the sound and video tracks as being two separate things which come together to make the experience of the viewer what it is. A well-done transition will be noticed by no one but will greatly improve their experience of the video. Poor transitions will be jarring and make it hard for your viewers to remain engaged in the video.

Sound can also make for effective transitions. An audio cue, like a phrase of music when you are transitioning from one section to another can punctuate your explanations in your videos. Sound effects like wooshes, or explosions can move you into the next section in an exciting, attention grabbing way.

Another really engaging way to do transitions is to edit to the music. Put your cuts on the beats or bars in your background music. This can lead to very impactful sequences of video, with the music and the visuals really working in concert to hook your viewer. You can often see where the beats and bars of music are happening by looking at the soundtrack waveform and cutting at those points. Otherwise simply listen to the music as the play head moves through your edit and leave marks where you want to cut, or listen and pause and cut when it seems right.

Stop motion and other animation.

Unless you are a seasoned animator, I would shy away from using animation for the bulk of your video creation. That's not to say there aren't ways to do animation quite quickly, but I suggest that you do your research and try a few things out before you commit to having every second of your videos complete with fun little animations.

However sometimes you come across something which is just better animated, there are a few ways to do this:

In editing software. You can create key frames and use motion, scaling or rotation to move things around on the screen in most editing software. You can even use 3D effects where you can anchor an object in the three-dimensional space of your video and have it move as the object moves. There are loads of ways to animate in editing software, they can be time consuming though and not the most intuitive.

Using PowerPoint animations. You are probably familiar with the animation features of *MS PowerPoint* so why not make animations in that software and just screen capture them being played back as a presentation, or even with timings and export a video. You can even playback the ink annotations you make in a presentation or exported video, which is awesome!

Try simple stop motion. Stop motion studio is the simplest app on smartphones for making stop motion animations. Use cut outs and move them around frame by frame to make fun attractive animations. All you really need is a way to keep the phone in the same place throughout. Or use *flip-a-clip* or any other app which lets you draw each frame over the ghost of the last so you can move any number of hand drawn objects around the screen. You could even use actual photographs to make a stop motion clip just by using the built in time-lapse (intervalometer) feature in cameras and just moving objects in between the photos being taken at five second intervals.

3. Making a brand

3a. Growing your Audience

Where audience meets with purpose is where community grows.

Knowing your audience is the first step to growing your audience. Think deeply and often about what content resonates and performs well with your target audience.

In the first chapter, titled "why you should try it" I wrote:

When you explain your purpose to your audience you begin to build the most powerful thing for YouTube growth: a community around your channel.

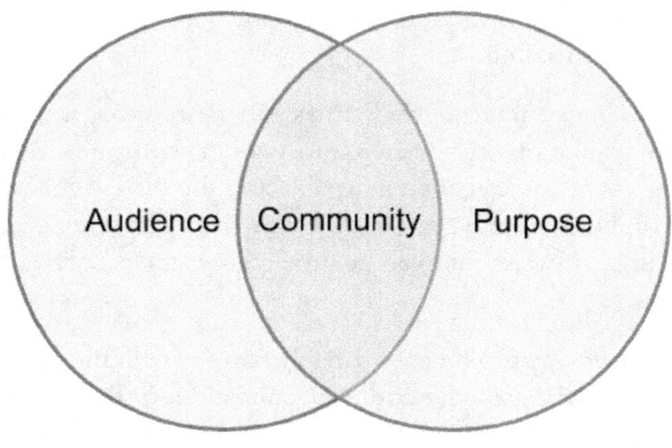

Where audience and purpose meet is where you build your community.

When people come together with shared goals, they form communities.

Communities on YouTube; contribute to the discussion and so the development of channels, they answer each other's queries, and they promote the channel by sharing on their own social medias or in their own real-life circles.

Communities around education channels.

I'd like to revisit that idea now and talk about the communities that arise around education YouTube channels.

They are usually changing as students sit exams at key times in their lives.

They are usually small and niche. There is a narrow band of people who are sitting the particular exam that you are teaching for, or who wish to study the topics that you cover at any given time. For this reason, it should be straight forward to know your audience and therefore to grow it!

However, they do not tend to want to watch every new video that you put out. They tend to use search to find answers to questions that they have, or explanations of topics that they are studying. They are not looking to watch every bit of content that you put out.

Understanding your community helps put your numbers in perspective. For example, don't compare your numbers to popular entertainment channels. The audience of an entertainment channel will tend to want to watch just about every video the channel puts out, regardless of its topic. The viewers know they are going to be entertained. Because of this the subscriber numbers are likely to be considerably higher than an education channel of a similar size.

Viewers of an education channel search for the answers that they want and aren't necessarily interested in everything that channel will put out. The trick then is to cover the content of your courses so that whenever they search for something in your subject, you have a video providing the answer. The audience that trust you will select your answer to their search query over the other options YouTube makes available to them.

Collabs are a great way to grow your audience

Collaborating with another channels of a similar size allows you to get access to a group of potential viewers who may not have been exposed to your channel. In most cases collaborating will mean making a video for each other's channels and uploading them to be shared with your followers. You can appear together, even without being together by planning and editing together something such that it feels like a discussion.

This works best if your audience is similar but you serve different values to them. For example, you both teach GCSE students, but different subjects.

Most of the time you should look to collaborate with channels of a similar size to your own. Don't expect that the very largest YouTuber in your niche is going to have the time to film something for your channel when you are just starting out. There's nothing wrong with reaching out though, they may just like your style and want to give you a boost.

Also, they may be interested in you making a video for their channel. Consider what you can offer and how it fits with their audience, purpose and value statement. You'll have the opportunity to plug your own channel in exchange for the content. Of course, you'll need to make sure that your production is good enough to sit alongside their production values on their videos.

Activity: Go to your analytics and sort the videos by views. Make a note of the 5 highest performing titles, make a note of the 5 lowest performing titles.

Now sort it by watch-time. Make a note of the 5 highest performing titles, make a note of the 5 lowest performing titles.

Look for any trends. Are there things that the highest performing videos have in common? Are there things that the lowest performing videos have in common?

Change the titles of the lowest performing videos, make a mental note to see if their performance increases in a few months' time.

Change your content strategy for the next three months to include only videos which have similar titles to your best performing videos.

Your aim in all this is not to please a search and discovery algorithm but to please the human being who is going to decide between your video and many other choices which will be presented to them at any given time.

I recommend doing this as you complete your first exam season of having a YouTube channel. Views and watch-time for exam focused educational content is much greater during the exam season, so give some of your videos the benefit of the doubt before then. If you released a video about good study habits just as schools were breaking up for Christmas holidays that video is likely to not have performed very well!

3b. Branding

Businesses and teachers.

Education business channels are different from teacher channels. As an education brand you will probably have access to a large team of people. You can collaborate to put out a large range of content which you publish at a regular cadence.

However even if you are a lone teacher looking to start making videos to enhance and complement your classroom practice it is still worth thinking about how you are beginning a brand on YouTube.

Branding your channel is a significant challenge, even if you already have an established brand with worldwide sales and a large website with lots of hits.

This chapter is about growing your brand *on YouTube*, even if you already have a brand identity established elsewhere, that needs to translate into the YouTube ecosystem. To be a success on YouTube your brand will need to behave differently to how it would behave on other social medias, or other forms of direct marketing. It will probably require a larger investment of time, but the rewards for success will be higher also.

If you need any proof of this, check the YouTube channels of any product that you see around the house. You'll see many have the YouTube logo on their social media icons on their branded packaging or their website. You'll be amazed at how low the numbers often are!

I am just one guy, making videos in my spare time, and my channel outperforms many multinational corporate brands who put huge budgets and teams behind their social media output.

The reason for that; *authenticity*.

Authentic Branding on YouTube.

It's often the case that an individual personality can provide a more authentic feel to a social media presence. Even when that presence is a large organization or even a multinational brand.

If you are making an education YouTube channel for a brand, I recommend that you find individual personalities in your organization to be the main personalities in your videos. This allows authentic storytelling, and what follows from that is authentic branding.

Even in a large pool of professionals you it can be hard to get quality videos produced and it can take a great deal of time. I sincerely recommend that you avoid corporate style videos on YouTube.

It's easy to think that because your organization can afford it then the best way to make your videos is to employ a professional production company. The videos they make look slick, but you'll pay far more than what they are worth. And the engagement in them in your in channel will be basically zero.

This is because you'll be getting the same video as everyone else. A professional media company doesn't know your company story, they aren't invested in the message and they don't know what is most compelling about your organization.

Find people who can tell good stories and make content that your audience can relate to and allow these personalities to grow on YouTube. Even if the initial quality of their videos isn't up to professional standards, they will be authentic. See this as a long game and as they learn, making better and better videos, the audience will grow with them.

You need to find out *who is going to be on camera?*

Run a competition. Give your employees either the activity from chapter 1c. "making your first video" or the making an explainer activity from chapter 2c. "types of video." Set a deadline and offer a prize.

Use these videos to find the personality. It doesn't even need to be someone super confident, just someone who can grow into the role. It doesn't need to be one person, but you do need to find a way to have a consistent style and tone. Most importantly find someone enthusiastic, who believes in your brand and is willing to learn how to make YouTube videos.

I see so many schools, colleges, education technology or other education brand make this mistake time and time again, and I cannot stress enough, *do not use the corporate style of video for YouTube.* You may wish to make one or two professional looking videos to auto play on your website, and these can look great and tell a very controlled message. But these videos will not grow your presence on YouTube. They do not engage an audience in your purpose. They will not create a community.

124

First the video needs to offer value.

Brands want to use YouTube for marketing. That is natural. They can see some individuals and companies making massive success of social media marketing and want a piece of the action.

The problem is, they too often enter the ecosystem with the idea that the videos are themselves advertisements for the products. You need to change the way around that you think about these videos compared to a traditional advert.

For your YouTube channel to grow, you need people to watch the *majority* of the videos. This means the video itself needs to have intrinsic value.

You can then, once you have an audience's attention, promote your product.

For example, the marketing message might be something like this:

This video gives you five essential study tips to help you prepare for the exams. But this book which you can buy from us gives you fifty study tips and a practical guide on how to get started revising!

When selling on YouTube the rule is:

The video offers value, the product offers ten times the value.

If you aren't interested in growing a YouTube channel with valuable content for its own sake, then consider just using your budget to sponsor channels that are making that type of content. You can pay to have a 30 second ad read within an already established creator in your niche. You'll get the same exposure, and you'll be supporting another educational professional.

These "sponsored videos" represent great value as you align your brand with a creator that already has an audience that trust them. You can get very good value per view of your ad read when compared to other forms of advertising. What is more is that if you choose the channel well you know that your adverts are very precisely targeted to the people that you want to reach.

Value proposition.

In chapter 1b "why you should try it" I introduced the idea of the *value proposition*. For branding on YouTube, this is everything. Your videos need to consistently deliver value and your audience will come back time and time again. Once they see your brand as the go to channel to provide that value, they will become willing to pay for it and they will be confident to buy it from you.

Ask yourself:

What problem do you solve for your audience?

And:

How do your videos solve that problem?

Identify the thing they should care about in your videos and hint on that at the beginning, middle and end of each of your videos. Using a small team of people to make and appear in all your videos makes it much easier to sew a consistent thread of your value proposition throughout your videos.

You see, what works on *Twitter*, or *Facebook*, or *Instagram* will not necessarily work on YouTube, and vice versa. YouTube isn't somewhere people go to flick, or comment, or interact with peers, they go for value, and they expect to have their attention held for longer periods of time.

YouTube is about stories and interpersonal connections. Think about the way you watch videos. It is a very intimate way to consume video on a small screen usually by ourselves.

It's good practice to have one (or very few) people who an audience gets to know and relates to. You need to find those people within your employees. Worry about the quality of the videos later, you just need to find keen and enthusiastic people with something to say for themselves on video as a start point.

Branding your logo, channel art and videos.

Branding needs to be consistent across all your output. At least it needs a consistent message. Before you go ahead and make your logo, channel name and thumbnails consider this most important question:

What's your unique selling point (USP)?

You may not be interested in selling anything. But if you want to be successful in any online space you must appreciate that you are selling *the click*. In exchange you are getting people's time and attention, and this is a very valuable commodity.

Considering what sets you apart should be central to the way that you brand your channel. Start with the name, make it give a clue as to the USP of your channel. It could be very directly about the subjects that you teach, or it could be purposefully different, and so hopefully memorable.

Channel art is largely the banner at the top of your channel homepage. It's not
the most important thing to get right because most of the traffic to your videos
will not come from your channel homepage. But it is a useful way to engage
people who have decided to subscribe to your channel. Consider how it looks,
whether it includes your slogan, or your value statement, or perhaps your
upload schedule, and perhaps the types of video viewers can expect to find on
your channel.

Brand your thumbnails. Try using a consistent background colour, or the same
font on each. You can include your logo on each if you like, although this
usually appears next to the title when the title and thumbnail are shown.
Perhaps there is a certain design that you can always use, for example, text
always in a circle background, or a coloured border or textured pattern.

Brand your videos. Using your logo, or slogan, or theme music or sounds.
Even your editing style or colour look adds commonality which eventually gets
associated with your brand. A cut screen you use between sections of your
video, a mascot, a background colour, pen colour, everything can key into your
brand.

Branding doesn't stop at the visuals though; your titles are part of the brand, as
is the content of the videos. *What types of things do you say? What topics do you
make videos on? What rituals or jokes do you make in your videos? In short, what is the
world like according to your brand?*

In the chapter "is it click bait" we discussed *the thing under the thing.* This is the
deeper meaning that pervades all of your channel content. It is the subtext
which drives the stories that you tell. And it is the relatable aspect of your
brand.

---

*Activity: Do your titles reflect your USP? Do your titles convey the deeper
meaning you want to associate with your brand?*

*Pick the three videos that are performing below average on your channel. Consider
whether the 100 character title ties in to the value proposition of your channel.*

*Change these titles and make a mental note to check back with them in a month
to see if viewing figures have increased. Do not change the title to be an inaccurate
description of the content of the video.*

3c. Understanding discoverability online

What do your audience search for?

The easiest way to get views when you are just starting out is to create good videos which show up in search. We discussed this at length on the chapter "categories of video".

However, finding a topic that sufficiently high numbers of people search for, but for which the competition isn't prohibitive of your video being chosen, is not necessarily an easy task. For example, a video aiming to teach people *how to draw a face,* will return thousands of results. As a new YouTube channel with a very small audience, you are unlikely to show up very high in the search if you choose this title. However *how to draw a happy face* may well be a title worth exploring.

A more closely focused niche is best for gathering initial momentum on YouTube, even if it may have a small volume of search traffic. As long as someone is out their searching for the topic of the video, if there is not a lot of competition that video will get views.

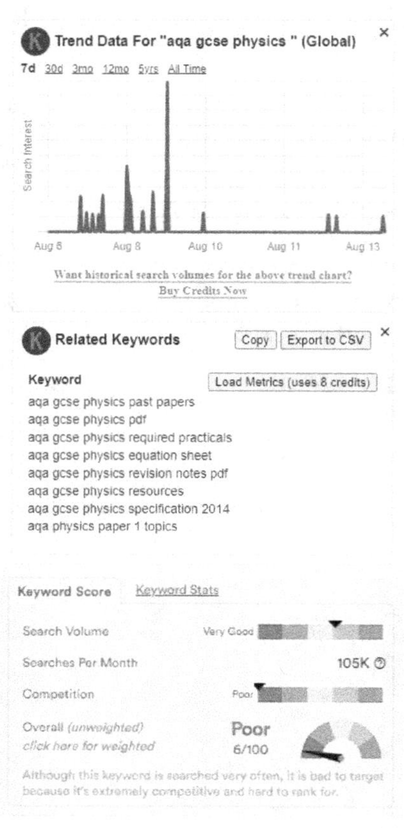

The process of researching your keywords is not a very glamourous or exciting one, but it is one of the strategies which is most likely to pay off when you are beginning to grow an education channel from zero views and zero subscribers.

The ideal search term to target would be one that has lots of searches but few results! There are tools out there such as *TubeBuddy* or *keywords everywhere*, or even the *Google keyword explorer* which will help you plan which keywords to target.

Keyword research will help you identify trends in your educational niche and to know the relative search volumes versus search results.

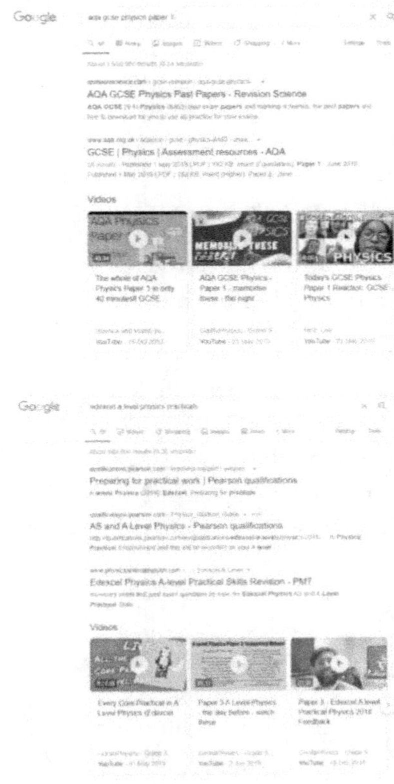

Even if your reach with your chosen search term is small, as long as someone finds your video and watches it, it will gather momentum and eventually get regular views.

A good *searchable* title will almost always be better for an education channel than a good *click bait* title will be. Especially whilst your reach is small, and you are learning how to sculpt watchable videos!

Search engine optimisation (SEO) is the process of making your videos more likely to show up in the search results for either Google Search or for YouTube's own search engine.

The gold standard for a SEO on YouTube is for a video to show up as one of the three videos displayed on the Google Search page for your target key word or key word phrase. If you can do this, then your video will get traffic. If you can get your videos into the top ten on YouTube search you will also be likely to be seen often enough to get traffic to your videos and enable your channel to grow.

Learn from and engage with other channels in your niche.

Imitation is the sincerest form of flattery. Looking closely at the successes of other channels in your educational niche can give you great insight into what works. It can give you good ideas for topics of videos that are successful with your audience and which you might not have thought of making.

You can get a video some traffic by positioning it next to other popular videos! You use this by making a video on a similar topic, with a similar title. Your keyword phrase can be similar to the keyword phrase that their video is targeting.

For example, if you notice a popular video entitled *five ways to study at home more effectively*, then a video entitled *five effective home study tips* will be likely to be suggested next to that video. This will work, and YouTube will suggest your video, providing you have made a quality video which people watch all the way through.

It's important not to copy their video, but it's ok to position your video as a "reaction to" video. For the example above, don't just give the same five tips, give your own five tips! Make five tips that you know will give value to your audience. Try and add value to the subject. Give your own take on the topic.

This isn't about spamming or trying to trick the algorithm into showing your video to people, it's about entering the conversation, and presenting your own value to a similar audience.

Moves like these have been shown to have huge success. There are lots of examples where a video mentions and discusses a much larger YouTuber and they are propelled to a much larger audience overnight. However, there are far more examples where a small YouTuber has mentioned a bigger one and the first few people who watched the video weren't interested in the actual content, so the video just died!

Where and how to share videos.

Where are these successful channels sharing their content? Then go and join them there. Engage with your audience wherever they can be found. Engage with your peers and YouTubers that you admire on all social platforms that you can. Not only will you get noticed by the YouTuber, but you will get noticed by their audience as well.

Go and comment on their videos, in the comments section your handle is your advert. If there is another channel that teaches your subject that is so big they haven't got time to answer all of the questions in their comments section, then you can go ahead and answer some for them. As long as the channel name that appears besides your comment makes it obvious that your channel offers a similar value to this one that they are engaging with, they will in all likelihood visit your channel and check you out.

Just don't be cynical about any of it. Go to comments sections and social medias expecting to get involved in a conversation around the topic of your educational niche. If you go there expecting to spam a link to your latest video, you will have no success in getting people to actually be interested in you. And besides, YouTube will probably hold any comment with a link for review as "likely to be spam."

Only post a link in response to someone if you are sure that the video that you are offering directly answers a question that someone is asking. For example, I am a keen user of *Twitter* for networking with other teachers, of Physics and of all subjects. I have found that many times I have a video that directly answers a question another user has asked. This type of tweet usually gets a much more positive reception than the few times I write an unsolicited tweet to promote my latest video.

Learn about SEO.

As with anything, the more you do keyword research the more you will learn about it.

One of the best things about *keywords everywhere*, *tube buddy* and *Google Keyword Explorer* is that they will teach you all about how to conduct and use keyword research and how to best optimise your content for search. I would also recommend a little-known website called *morning fame*, even just by doing their free trial I was able to learn loads about the process of trying to pick video topics and how to make them more likely to rank highly in search results.

The more you try to optimise your videos and their metadata for search the more you will learn about SEO. You will also start to gain a *feel* for what is going to work for your videos and your channel. You'll start to get an understanding of what your audience searches for and what they will click on when presented to them.

The YouTube search algorithm rewards relevance more than anything. So it will, other indicators being equal, present a more closely matched title and content higher in the search ranking. This means that you should keep your search orientated videos as focussed on the keyword phrase topic as possible.

Remember also that YouTube reads everything it can about your video, including the title of the file you upload and the autogenerated, (or uploaded), transcript of the content of the video! But the most highly weighted metadata for search, and so the ones you should focus on the most, is the title and the first few lines of the description.

Activity: Try following this simple SEO checklist for a few video uploads and reflect on how much it impacts the viewing figures for your videos.

1. Say the keyword phrase at least three times in the video itself.

2. Make the video file that you upload the same name as your keyword phrase.

3. Write a title which includes the keyword phrase naturally.

4. Include the keyword phrase in the first lines of the description.

5. Either upload your transcript to the subtitles tab of your video, or check and correct the accuracy of the auto generated subtitles.

Trends.

When you notice trends in your niche it's imperative for channel growth that you jump on them and get some content out as soon as possible. I'd suggest using live feeds to respond to emerging trends. Live feeds take very little preparation and zero post processing. If you get a good idea of something you want to say, jot down a quick overview of the video, switch on the camera and go for it.

You can see live feeds as a low investment, low jeopardy way to test out an idea. If you've got an idea for a title that you think will get clicks, try it. It might become one of your most popular videos, or it might get less than a hundred views and go nowhere. But you won't have invested much time!

I have, in the past spent entire holidays working on content that I hoped would be popular and which have had very few views. If only I had just shoved it out there as a live feed. I'd know that it wasn't going to be popular and could have used the same time to work on videos that are proven to work with viewers of my channel.

Suggested vs discoverable vs subscriber content.

There are basically three ways videos get discovered:

Suggested: These are views that have come from YouTube deciding that based on a viewer's behaviour and interests that they will likely want to watch your video. The algorithm has presented them with your thumbnail and title and the viewer has decided to watch your video.

Search: These views have come up as a result of your video being shown in the search results for a particular query. You can go deeper into the analytics to find out what exact search terms which are being used to find your videos and you can prioritise the most popular ones in your upcoming videos.

Direct: These are views where someone has come to your video via a link. This could have been from a website, from a document, email or social media. (It could also have been from google, which kind of makes it a search view in any case!) Again, you can go into more detail to discover exactly what the website sources were.

We discussed ways to think about how you can make your videos more likely to be discovered in these ways in the chapter "categories of videos." We also talked about how the content of the video should be different because the person arriving to the video will have different amounts of knowledge about your channel and different expectations of the video.

Pay attention to the changes in traffic sources during a typical year. Try to understand *how and why the traffic sources vary*. And also, *how and why the search terms vary*.

For example, on my channel, in spring and summer 2020, during the Covid-19 lockdown and school closures, direct traffic increased, whereas search traffic decreased. I think that this is because instead of students searching for revision materials, they were being set links to my videos by other teachers for use in distance learning.

I also noticed during this time a large shift from search terms like *GCSE Paper 1* or *how to revise effectively* to terms about specific content, for example *alpha, beta and gamma* or *radioactivity*. This is because instead of my audience preparing for exams, they were interested in learning particular topics for the first time.

Earlier in the book I talked about subscriber numbers on education channels not being as good an indicator as to the health of the channel. Your watch-time on your channel is a better metric to focus on. This is because of the importance of the suggested video or the YouTube homepage feed.

Most viewers don't look through the subscription tab of their YouTube app. Most viewers just scan through their home tab, which is like a news feed on any other social media. This is different for every viewer. Presenting you with things that YouTube has calculated that you will be interested to watch. If you want to grow quickly on YouTube, you need to start being suggested on individuals home pages and in their home feeds.

As users on YouTube we often have so many subscriptions that we aren't actually interested in seeing everything that every channel we subscribe to puts out. Because of this you should increase your call to action to include asking viewers not just to subscribe, but to have notifications turned on. This will mean that they get a notification every time you publish a video or start live streaming. This can drastically increase the numbers of viewers who see your videos within the first few hours and so can make your videos more likely to be promoted by the algorithm.

This is one more reason why you should focus on improving your CTR and your watch-time as a priority. Perhaps focus on writing titles which have all the elements to entice your audience to click, all in fifty characters or less; that way all the title will be shown in the news feed on mobile devices.

Where views come from.

The traffic source metric in your analytics panel can tell you loads about how people are finding your videos. Some of the ways your videos are discovered may surprise you! Spend time analysing the trends of how people discover your videos and use them to strategize and optimise your content for upcoming videos. You'll find this detail in the "analytics / reach" section of YouTube studio.

Most importantly think about what the sources tell you about who is watching and try to plan the content of the video accordingly. For example, a video which has most of the traffic coming from search is probably going to be being viewed by people who haven't seen your channel much before. Including a plug for your products, or a lengthy update on your channel video schedule is probably not going to keep them watching!

Here is a quick run through of the traffic sources that you'll see in the analytics of your videos. I'll tell you what you should learn from each if this traffic source is the largest of the sources, and what you can do as a result of that information to maximise the number of views which come through that source.

Search: This video is getting a lot of its views through search. People are typing relevant key terms into the YouTube search box and finding this video. Check your title and description prominently contain the search terms that people are using to find this video. Do a bit of keyword research to find popular related searches to this topic, add those terms into the metadata if they are representative of the content. Consider planning other videos to answer this and related search queries in the future.

Browse: Videos that are being found by browse features are probably people subscribed, or who have seen and enjoyed your videos in the past. These are the people to show your fun side to. Build up a few rituals in these videos. Ask them for comments, to submit questions, to share your videos or to buy merch. These are the people that your community will grow from! Engage them in your channel and its journey.

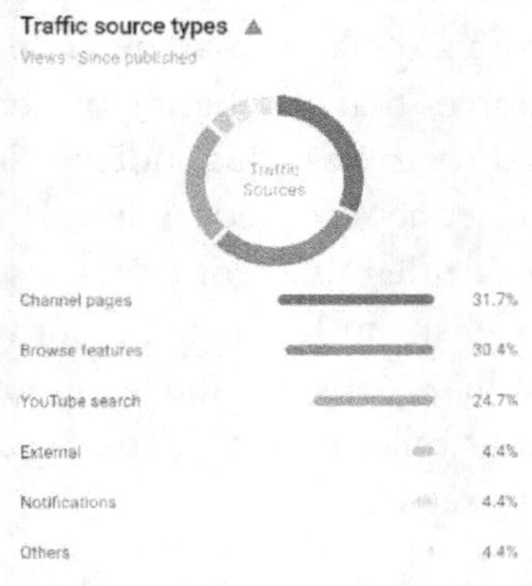

Channel Pages: These are views that have come from people looking through the content on your channel. In other words these are people that were on your channel page, looked through and selected this video. You can see this as a similar type of viewer to the *browse* source. These are engaged viewers, who are either returning to your channel or having a good dig around because they feel like it is something for them.

Suggested: This is the traffic source that you should prioritise if rapid growth is important to you. It is not easy to make this the main source for your video, but if you are successful in placing your video around a topic which has a large number of people interested in it then, as long as people who view your video watch the majority of it, YouTube will suggest it to the side of videos, or after videos, or in the home feed. Consider making the title and thumbnail of the video more shareable to encourage viral growth of the video.

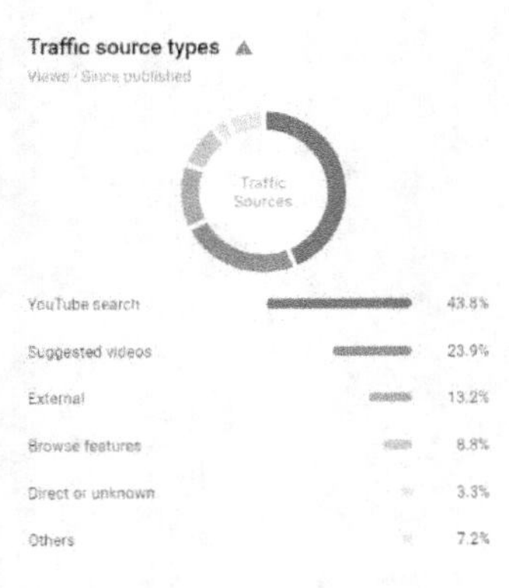

External: These are videos that are getting a lot of views from webpages and sources from outside of YouTube. Make sure you look a little deeper, one video which has a lot of external views may be coming from *Twitter* and the other mostly from *Google*. You should see them as separate sources. By looking a little deeper into the analytics, I can see that this video's external sources were largely from search engines. You should treat this the same as if it were a majority search traffic source.

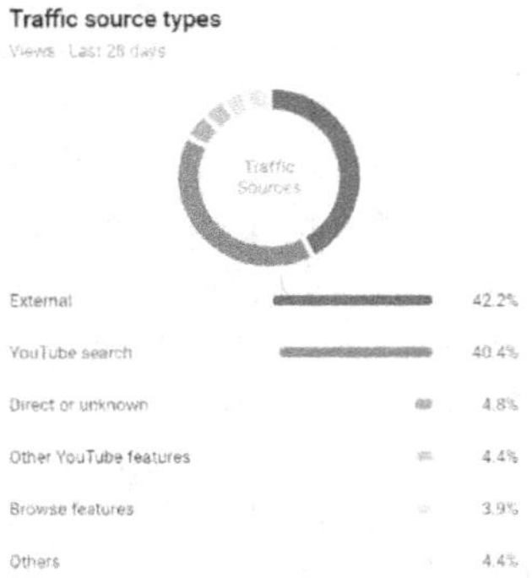

However if you see that the external source is from a social media, then consider finding the sources that are sharing on the social platform and try to bear this audience in mind for subsequent related topics. If for example you notice that many of the views are coming from a website in India, great, but you should perhaps consider adding subtitles to the video, and similar future videos to ensure YouTube can translate the video more accurately.

Some of my videos have homework websites, or university web pages a large external source. This tells me that the video is valued by teachers more than students. I might consider the style of that video and emulate it again in other videos I wanted to get in front of the facilitators of learning rather than the students.

Activity: Look at the analytics for several recent videos which have performed above average in terms of numbers of views. Find the metric "traffic sources" and analyse whether the content and meta data is suitable for the types of viewers that you are likely to have received. Ask yourself if there is anything particular that you did differently for a video with, for example, a significant proportion of views coming through search, or a significant proportion of views coming through suggested traffic sources.

Look at the search terms that have been used to reach your videos which have come from a majority search traffic source. Think about the viewpoint of the person who is discovering this video in that way. Plan a video on a similar topic and design the thumbnail, title and content to appeal directly to the person you imagine discovering your video through search.

Now look at a video which has had a majority of its views through suggested videos. Think about the experience of a person discovering this video who has no experience of your channel. Now plan a video around a similar topic and try to appeal to someone for whom this is the first experience of your channel.

Finally look for a video which has a majority of its views coming through browse features. These are likely to be viewers who have watched and enjoyed your content before. Ask yourself why these viewers enjoyed this video more than other videos on similar topics you've released in the past. Plan a video on a similar topic which a returning viewer will be likely to watch all the way through.

Activity: Look at the last five titles to your videos. How are these videos going to be found? Will they be found as the result of search terms or discovery. Unless you have a large online presence to push traffic to your videos you had better find a way to get your videos found!

Next ask yourself how popular a search term is it that you are targeting? Are you likely to get noticed ahead of the other videos that cover the topic. If there are lots of videos from much bigger channels then you are unlikely to be in the top ten results in search, so you are unlikely to gain many views.

There are two ways to reduce this issue, either make your target search terms more specific. For example; there may be millions of videos on "cells" on YouTube, but there may only be three which are specifically designed to teach students who are studying a particular course, from a particular exam board. This is your route into higher rankings on search.

Try changing the titles of a few of your videos which are not performing well in search to make them more specific. Consider adding things like qualification, exam board or even grades or levels.

3d. Writing a YouTube Strategy

Audience = Strategy

YouTube will promote your videos without you doing anything if you get the strategy right! The strategy will be right if the value proposition that you make is prominent in all of your content and that it is accurately matched to the interests of your audience.

Your first task when you are writing a strategy is to define who your audience is. Don't so much think about demographics, as define something that they want that links every member of your intended audience.

For example, for *GorillaPhysics* my audience is; committed students looking for ways to ensure they get the highest grades possible. My value proposition is; *GorillaPhysics teaches you how to get the A*.*

Your intended audience should be the first and last thought when you are writing a content strategy. You need to know what they search for and what they need. Your strategy should you direct them around your content. Plan into it how each video links to the next and how they all link back to your core value proposition.

For example, I know that my audience look for easy ways to get the highest grades. They want *the trick* to getting full marks on exam papers. But I know that they need detailed advice on how and what to study, they need accurate tutorials and they need exam technique. What I try to do in my strategy is to give them what they need, dressed up as what they want.

Your strategy should be a planned schedule of production and uploads. It should consist of a balance of the three categories of videos, and all should be linked by the *audience* and *value proposition.*

The activity in this chapter is going to give you a format for you to start planning your content strategy. This is not to say that this is all you should consider when planning out your content for the next three months, or the next year, but it is a good structured start.

This is also not to say that a good strategy shouldn't include just trying out a new idea, popping up on a live feed because you've got something interesting to say that you think your audience want to hear, or smashing out a quick and dirty phone video based on what you are up to today. But you should get into the habit of calmly thinking through all the options periodically as you develop your channel. You want to achieve consistency and coherence, and this tends to come from reflection, and strategizing.

What they look for vs what they need.

Consider how your audience uses the videos that you make, or that already exist in your niche. For example, if you know that videos in your niche that are very popular tend to be longer for lecture style videos, consider giving them the same. Or if you know that channels in your niche tend to have audience participation in the form of video responses to questions asked by the audience, go for this. Or, if you know better, then give them something different and explain why the way that you are breaking the mould is in fact better than what they know and love.

Try to give actual meaningful advice, but know that you need to meet them in the environment that already exists on YouTube. For my audience it is the study-tube environment of pastel highlighters and beautiful note taking, the world of memes around exams, and exam board fails, sit down chats, Q&As and study-with-me videos. This is all really good and is a warm environment, but I can't produce that form of content; they don't want a life update from a *teacher*! But I can make reference to these things, I can consider the stationary that I use and try to make calm purposeful tutorials, which provide an air of similarity to the ecosystem in which my channel exists.

You are the authority on your subject and your viewers are coming to you to learn. Don't be afraid to direct them. Make well planned routes through the material that you make. Playlists are a great way to organise this on your channel homepage or organising them on your own website is also a great idea.

You need to guide and nurture their aspiration. For example, think about carrying the audience you create on a journey through from GCSE to A level to University. Help signpost their way, and the more you think about them and try to meet their needs and expectations, the more they will grow in number and investment in you, your channel and your brand.

Remember as educator you can facilitate great learning by providing great content, but you can also direct their studies by telling them how to study effectively, or giving them examples from your experience of how students have been successful in your subject in the past.

Check the value matches the audience.

Remember that the value you offer is central to the content. The content itself should provide value. For example, if you are using your educational channel for marketing purposes make sure that the *videos offer value and the products offer ten times the value.* Even if you have no physical product to sell, consider that you are selling the next engagement, the next click, the next investment in you and your channel. If you want growth, at the very least, you are selling the subscribe button!

When you are defining what that value is for your channel, you need to consider closely how that value matches the person that you have defined for your audience.

Your strategy should answer the question; *what problem do you solve for your audience?* It might be that you guide students through the year, or that you enable their hobby, or that you are the one reference they are going to need to make sure they get their highest grade in the exams.

Try to think about the value proposition as more than just *to learn about*…. Try to make it a statement which ties together your *USP*, your *thing under the thing* and the *motivation of your audience.*

If you know that you want to produce videos for two different audiences then consider whether you should have two channels. The two different audiences might be teachers and students, otherwise they may be students but split by age range. This is more manageable if you are an education brand or company that has more person power.

Channels run by individuals have the benefit of being unified around the individual, so even if there are two or three categories, or streams of content intended for different audiences, or to be consumed in different ways, they make sense on the same channel because of the personality.

Don't forget that the value proposition can be you and your personality.

Try to include your value proposition in every video at the beginning, and end, and ensure that your content delivers on this.

When you periodically review your strategy, check whether your value matches your audience. *Are they actually engaging? Is the content solving problems for them? Are they getting the intended value from your content?*

Chat with viewers, respond to comments and requests. Ask them in the video to tell you what they want next. Ask them what they think of these types of videos that you are making. Ask them how you could better cater for their needs.

Comments are signals of engagement for YouTube. And engagement on the platform makes your content worth promoting.

Write and re-write your value proposition. Say it out loud. Imagine it as a sound bite and refine it as you go.

Audience.

Value proposition. Include in every video (at beginning).

10x value. Include in every video (at end).

Searchable videos (discovery). SEO
1.
2.
3.
4.
Easiest to get views when just starting.

Suggested videos (returning viewers)
1.
2.
3.
Easiest to get views when you have YouTube presence

Hero videos (direct from website or app) controlled message
1.
2.
Easiest to get viewers if you have other large online presence

Strategy responds to the audience.

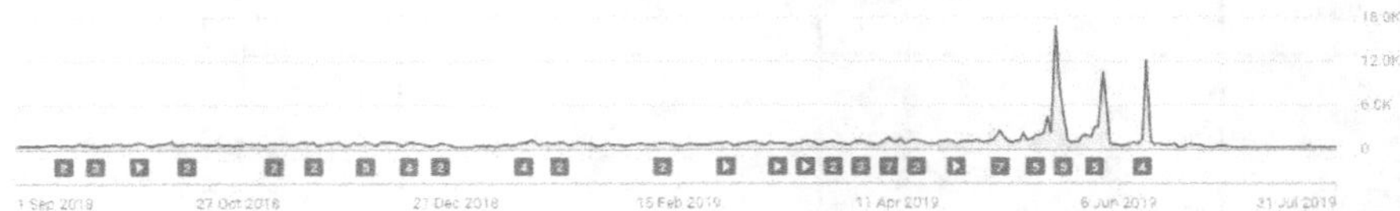

This graph is the viewing figures on my channel for the 18/19 academic year.

You can see steady engagement throughout the year at around a thousand views per day and then massive spikes which are the nights before key exams! Also notice; basically zero views during the Christmas and summer holidays! You can also see the numbers of videos in each week that I published. Increasing in frequency to almost daily during the build up to exam season.

When you are writing your content strategy think about the year in education. Of course, this will vary depending on location, but for UK schools the year looks something like this:

month	September	October	November
school events	New school year starts.	Busy, churning through content.	Winter, low feelings grinds, students and teachers are tired. Mock exams!
message	Start as you mean to go on. Stationery. Good habits. Study skills. Buy materials.	Teaching content. Things from examiners reports. Get discovered.	Whole paper videos. Exam questions. Exam technique.
month	**December**	**January**	**February**
school events	Winding down, festive fun, this is far enough from exams.	A Level mock exams.	Ski trips! Sick of the message about how important the year is.
message	How to find gaps. How to learn from exam papers.	New resolutions. Study planners. Set goals.	Whole papers. Teaching content. Hard bits.

month	March	April	May
school events	Mock Exams.	Easter.	Exams.
message	Reassurance. Nerves. How to prioritise.	Get a head of your peers. Get exam focused. Live streams.	Find the dates, avoid the nights before exams not in the subject. Live streams the night before.
month	June	July	August
school events	Exams.	Summer Holidays.	Results days.
message	Half term re-focus. Confidence. Hard bits. Q&As.	(Take a break and strategize for next year, learn from your analytics.)	Results live. Starting Uni. Starting 6th form.

Your message has to change to reflect the change in your audience. Perhaps make a table similar to this and plan out how your content and your message will change through the year.

Ask yourself questions like: *What is current, what is trending in your area? What will your audience click through on, right now?*

Once you've been developing your channel for a year, and produced a variety of videos on various topics, you analyse how your audience's habits change throughout the year. A good strategy will use this to plan the topics and types of content that you put out in each month.

Live streams are especially good for adding watch time and for getting noticed. YouTube is more likely to promote a live stream during the broadcast than a pre-recorded video with a similar title. If you can get your titles right and be delivering the value you promised when someone clicks, it's a great way to build an audience when you are starting out. Plan them into your strategy.

They are a great way to respond to what is happening now in your niche or subject area. They are also a great way to build audience engagement. Perhaps you do take the brave decision to include a Q&A in a live stream, but maybe you also ask for feedback. Ask the audience what type of videos they want to see from you in the near future. Use live streams to be responsive to your audience!

144

How to go viral.

Whilst I would say that I have never really had a truly viral video. More than one of my videos has gone *micro-viral*. That is to say that the number of views has increased in the hundreds per hour for a sustained period of days.

Viral videos emerge because of two things, they *hit upon some trend* that many people are interested in at that particular time and that they are *inherently shareable*. Want to guess what trend I hit upon?

Honestly, I was trying to make a physics video about conservation of angular momentum....

Oh well, my most popular video, and not at all one of my best!

People make entire livings just trying to make viral video content. They have many more misses every time they get a hit. *Casey Neistat* explains that he has had many viral hits, but that he cannot tell you how to make a viral video. Just how to make a video that has the potential to go viral.

Something that <u>interests people at that time</u>, *spinners in 2016,* something which has the <u>potential to be shared</u>, *how they work*.

As it was growing, I looked at the analytics for this video. I noticed that many of the views were coming from direct links from social medias and from one children's website written in Lithuanian!

The thing was that I tried to re-emulate this afterwards, with more videos on spinners, all the time trying to make them interesting to as wide a group of people as possible and also trying to make them have titles and content that people would want to share. These follow-up videos did ok, but nowhere near the first one. You see there is no way to guarantee your video to be shared and go viral, just ways to make it more likely to be shared. It's always going to be a hit and miss video tactic!

Activity: Try a keyword phrase that you are considering for the title of your next video. Look at the three videos presented by google on the google search results for that page.

Which channels are they from? If they are from large popular channels with high production values then you are unlikely to be able to break into the top three video results for this search. If this is the case try narrowing the search terms by adding more specific detail to the key word phrase.

Once you have found specific keyword phases to target, include them in your next videos following the good SEO practices we established in the chapter "understanding discoverability online". But also try to adapt the content and title to make it more likely to be sharable. Try to naturally include your target keyword phrase, but in a way which makes it seem more compelling to a wider audience.

Check how your video performs in search by searching for your target keyword phrase into a browser that you are not signed into. This is because google and YouTube use cookies to tailor your search results to you, so you will not see a true reflection of the search results everyone else will see!

3e. Analytics: which bits matter? And what does it all mean?

Learn how to keep people watching.

By far the most important metric to learn from is the audience retention graphs. This is because if one thing is true on YouTube:

If you get people to watch the majority of your video, it will do well.

The aim of YouTube is to have viewers watch for as long as possible. This may seem like a less than noble aim but remember that YouTube is a business. Like any other business, YouTube needs to make money, and that money comes from ad revenue. The more people watch YouTube the more advertisement slots there are to sell to companies. For this reason, YouTube will promote a video if they can be confident that people will actually watch it.

Increasing watch time therefore, increasing the audience retention, should be your number one goal, and it should be the first thing that you look at in your analytics in terms of performance. Remember that you are a part of that business and YouTube wants to reward you by giving you a cut of that advertising revenue!

It is easy to focus on views and subscribers and think that these numbers are the most important thing to try to increase. It's a bit like the writer, who complains that people would surely love their book if they actually bothered to read past the first chapter! Focus on watch time and the views and subscribers will follow.

If you find that your videos are underperforming, your first thought should always be to try to improve your videos. Don't blame other factors that you cannot control and don't despair. Just see it as part of the learning process.

You don't need to take down an underperforming video, or re-record it, just try and make the next one better.

Audience retention graphs.

Here are three audience retention graphs and what they tell me about the video. Notice firstly that all of them have roughly the same average watch time, around a minute and a half. This is quite low for my channel, but the percentage viewed, and the shape of the audience retention graph tells a more interesting story.

Notice also that all of them have a steep fall off in the first few seconds of the video. Again, this is normal on YouTube, many people abandon videos in the first few seconds because of things like auto-play, or they selected something from their suggested videos and then quickly changed their minds.

The thing to be interested in is what happens after this initial dip. These are the people who have actually decided to watch the video. If they choose to stay to the end, you are doing something right.

This video is not performing well. People start the video, but it quickly fails to deliver what they were expecting.

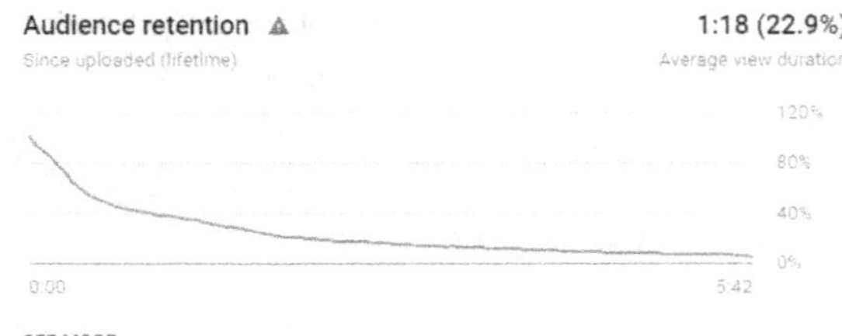

This video is doing ok, on average they stay for >50%. But around 80% decide to watch the video but for some reason they start to leave around 35s in. I can learn from what I did at this time in the video.

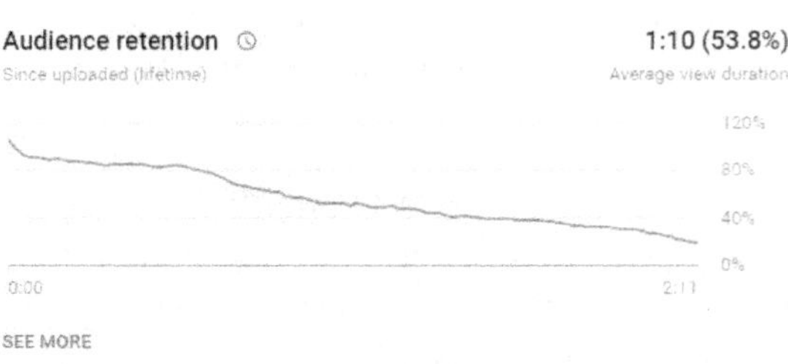

This video is doing well. Those who chose to stay do stay for well over half of the video. It is one of my highest performing videos. They start to leave when I say *thanks for watching!*

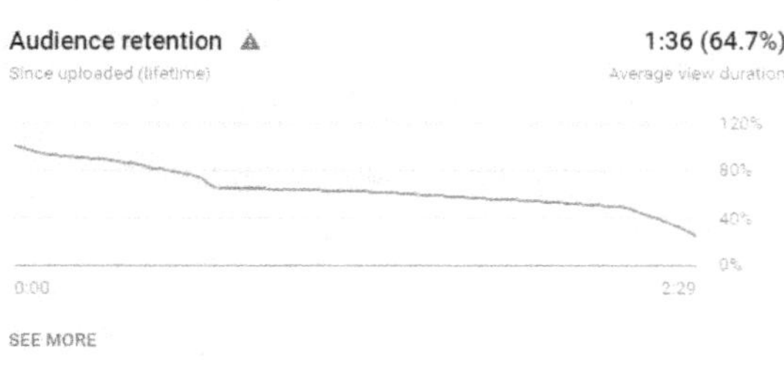

There is nothing that YouTube wants more than a flat audience retention graph. Even if the numbers are low, if people stay to the end, YouTube will try and match the video to those people!

Watch time.

Remember that above all else, "watch time" is the key indicator of the health of your channel. YouTube switched to this metric after clickbait thumbnails were becoming ubiquitous in the middle of the last decade. The thumbnails promised one thing and the video delivered something completely different. This was undermining the credibility of the platform.

Before they changed to using watch time as a measure of the worth of the video, they used views. So, a video with a clickbait title and thumbnail could get loads of views, but no one watched for longer than fifteen seconds! Humans do not put up with online environments that are not delivering what they promise for very long. Using watch time gives the YouTube algorithm a firmer understanding of the quality of the video content.

They released a visual metric that we call the funnel, and it really sums up how the algorithm works in terms of videos. Simply put, the wider the base of your funnel, the healthier your channel.

This is the funnel from a calendar year of my channel.

Impressions and how they led to watch time

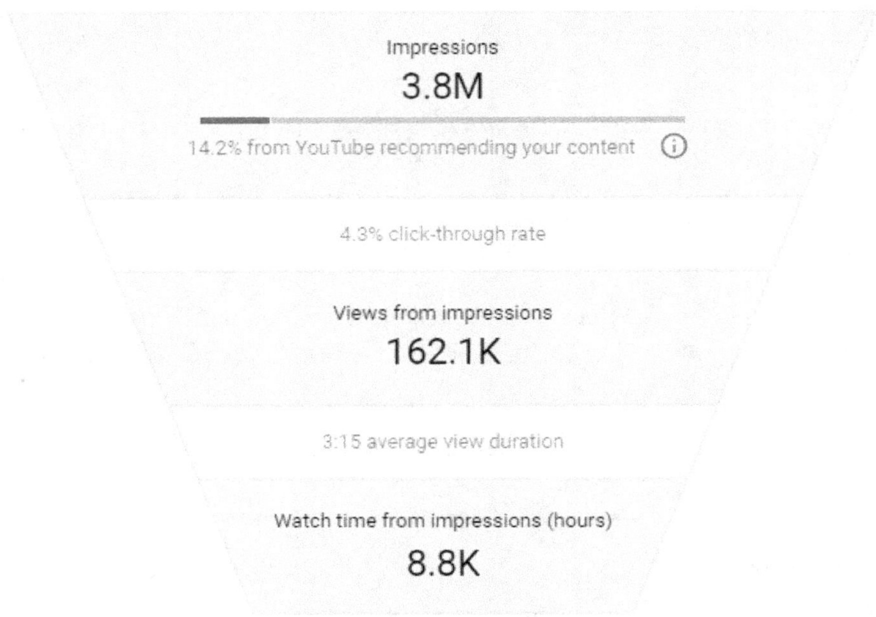

From top to bottom the funnel shows:

1. How many times YouTube displayed your title and thumbnail, either in search or suggested. You can see the majority of my impressions come from search. I need to improve the percentage of times YouTube is recommending my content.
2. The click through rate (CTR). A measure of how effective your titles and thumbnails are in getting people to choose to watch them. My CTR is ok, probably about average for YouTube. I have worked hard to improve my titles and thumbnails for this measure.
3. The actual numbers of views that this leads to. Note this excludes direct traffic to your videos by links. My channel gets quite a few direct links as my videos are linked by teachers in homework and appear in other educational websites reasonably often.
4. The average view duration. This is quite high for an educational channel like mine, but I'm always trying to improve this score!
5. The total watch time from YouTube showing my titles and thumbnails. This is not bad; it equates to 367 days of watch time! A whole year of watch time, in a calendar year!

To sum up the message of the funnel; *watch time is the key to YouTube suggesting your content.* The longer people spend watching your videos, the more likely YouTube is to recommend them.

It is a record of all the times YouTube showed your thumbnail and title to someone and how long they watched in total.

Other metrics and what you can learn from them.

Here I've described a few key indicators that you might notice in your analytics. Look out for these as they can indicate whether your channel is healthy or not. I've then written what should you learn from these indicators. Try to use these indicators to give you ideas, to try new things and to improve your videos.

You have a low click through rate (CTR). Your video appears in search, but people don't click on it. Consider improving your thumbnails and titles.

People are leaving your video in the first few moments. You are not delivering what your title and thumbnails promised in first few moments. It is an indication that people realise that it is not what they were looking for.

Your audience retention is lower than 50%. You're failing to hold their attention, either your video is not engaging enough, you aren't delivering value to them, or you aren't inspiring confidence. Look out for particular points in the video where they drop out. Try to avoid these things in the next videos you make.

Some of your videos perform much better than others. Try and learn from the type or category which performs well and consider why the other videos do not perform well. It may be that the content was ok, but something about the video did not engage, or was not searchable. Try and repeat the things which are positive and learn to avoid the negatives. Importantly use success and failures to learn what your audience want.

Different times of year you have much better viewing figures. This is normal. Try to understand how a year looks in your niche. For some videos timing is important and other videos will be slow burners which get constant traffic from search. Consider using live streams to respond to trends.

Your retention curve is pretty flat. This is a good sign, every video on YouTube will have some immediate drop off on retention, you shouldn't worry too much about this as it is largely due to auto play. But if most people who decide to stay with your video do stay, this is a good sign. Your video represents value for someone, and that's what ultimately will lead to success.

3f. Finally…

Always be ~~educating~~ learning.

Remember the game changes. The advice in this book might not be great advice in a few years' time. Something else may have taken the place of YouTube as the go to place to learn new skills and for young people to watch teacher explainer videos. But the hope is that by going on this journey, you've learned some skills to allow you to take advantage of the next change in digital learning!

Hopefully you'll have fun too…. I hope that you'll put some of this into practice and enjoy learning how to make great videos. Please do pop up and let me know how it is going. And remember, just like at the front of a classroom, nothing is more engaging than a big smile!

Keep yourself grounded in the aims that you had at the beginning. At least stay grounded if they were modest aims! If you have started YouTube with the most ambitious aims, keep in touch with those too, and use them to keep you focused and determined to reach your goals.

Start YouTube knowing at the very least it will change your classroom practice. Know that it's good for your own revision, and your own professional development. And know that you will reach people and you will teach them something, and they will be grateful for your time and efforts. I hope for you, as it is for me, that in itself will be enough of a reward.

For me I've always found YouTube works best when I've been able to integrate it into my own teaching. What I mean by that is that I've been able to film bits in lessons or shortly after lessons. When I've just taught something, I've got a really clear explanation in my head because I've just had to present it to people! It's a great way to appear more fluent in your videos.

I've made a lot of popular videos on my walk to school and I've done live streams about things that I was thinking about that day, or that I've presented to classes or in assemblies. I'd encourage you if you are starting YouTube to think about it as not being separate from you normal teaching practice. Integrate it into your practice.

I'm a lone teacher making videos in my spare time I've had more than a million views. Sure, not all of them have stayed the entire way through the video. But on average they have watched two videos. That's five hundred thousand individuals. Ok so many of them just watched a little bit of one video. So maybe it's more like fifty thousand engaged people, you have actively used my videos to study physics. That statistic blows my mind every time! I'm grateful for each and every one of them. It makes me so pleased that I have spent the time I have in developing my channel.

Make content for yourself.

Make content that you know *you'll* be proud of in years to come. Make content that is authentic to *you*.

Enjoy making videos to spread factual information, videos for reference and videos for community. I think the more of us that can use audio visual media to spread good, reliable information can only be a good thing in the post-fact age of misinformation!

I've written a great deal about catering for an audience in this book. Why not have the single thing that drives your audience, the defining criteria that makes them your audience *because they are like you.*

YouTube allows you to be intimate and personable. The audience may seem distant when it is just the camera and you, mumbling over your words and thinking about what to say next. But they are not so distant when they watch.

I think it's why we love it so much, that YouTube allows us to put ourselves out there, and find an audience who will consume everything that you post.

Any more questions….

If you have any more questions about teaching on YouTube, I'd be really pleased to hear from you. I'm @GorillaPhysics on *Twitter* or otherwise my email address is kit@gorillaphysics.com. Please do get in contact, I'm really keen to grow my network of teachers and educators who are interested in online learning and making educational videos.

If you liked the book, please let everyone know by leaving a 5-star review. If you didn't like it, please let me know. I really am always keen to read constructive criticism.

Thanks for reading, come over and subscribe to *GorillaPhysics* on YouTube, and let me know how else I can help.

Activity: I want to make an offer to you. Subject to availability, (as I have said, I am full time father of two, husband and Head of Science!)

If you would like to arrange a video call where we can look through your channel, its analytics and your content strategy then please email and we can arrange this.

If you are a teacher, like me, just making content in your spare time then I offer this **45minute call, free of charge.** *For education companies and brands looking for the same service, please get in contact to discuss what my time is worth to you.*

I know that by looking in detail at your channel and your aims on YouTube together, we can come up with some strategies to help you grow your audience, and educate more people in your niche.
